THE SHOOTING SCRIPT ™

THE TRUMAN SHOW

THE TRUMAN SHOW

SCREENPLAY, FOREWORD, AND NOTES BY
ANDREW NICCOL

INTRODUCTION BY
PETER WEIR

A Newmarket Shooting Script™ Series Book
NEWMARKET PRESS • NEW YORK

10 9 8 7 6 5 4 3 2 1

Library of Congress Cataloging in Publication Data available upon request

ISBN 1-55704-367-1

QUANTITY PURCHASES
Companies, professional groups, clubs, and other organizations
may qualify for special terms when ordering quantities of this title.
For information, write Special Sales, Newmarket Press,
18 East 48th Street, Suite 1501, New York, New York 10017,
or call (212) 832-3575, or fax (212) 832-3629.

Manufactured in the United States of America

OTHER NEWMARKET SHOOTING SCRIPTS™ INCLUDE

Merlin: The Shooting Script
U-Turn: The Shooting Script
Swept from the Sea: The Shooting Script
The People vs. Larry Flynt: The Shooting Script
Dead Man Walking: The Shooting Script

The Birdcage: The Shooting Script
The Shawshank Redemption: The Shooting Script
A Midwinter's Tale: The Shooting Script
The Age of Innocence: The Shooting Script

OTHER NEWMARKET MOVIEBOOKS INCLUDE

The Seven Years in Tibet Screenplay and Story Behind the Film
Men in Black: The Script and the Story Behind the Film
The Age of Innocence: A Portrait of the Film Based on the Novel by Edith Wharton
The Sense and Sensibility Screenplay & Diaries
Showgirls: Portrait of a Film
Panther: A Pictorial History of the Black Panthers and the Story Behind the Film
Mary Shelley's Frankenstein: The Classic Tale of Terror Reborn on Film
Bram Stoker's Dracula: The Film and the Legend

Dances with Wolves: The Illustrated Story of the Epic Film
Far and Away: The Illustrated Story of a Journey from Ireland to America in the 1890s
Gandhi: A Pictorial Biography
The Inner Circle: An Inside View of Soviet Life Under Stalin
City of Joy: The Illustrated Story of the Film
Neil Simon's Lost in Yonkers: The Illustrated Screenplay of the Film
Last Action Hero: The Official Moviebook
Rapa Nui: The Easter Island Legend on Film
Wyatt Earp: The Film and the Filmmakers
Wyatt Earp's West: Images and Words

CONTENTS

FOREWORD

BY ANDREW NICCOL

I first met Mr. Peter Weir in a hotel room in Los Angeles, where I found him to be a deeply disturbed and paranoid man. Naturally, I was thrilled.

His talent as a filmmaker had never been in question but the fact that he came close to sharing some of my own afflictions, I knew then that the script was in excellent hands.

The question that I am most often asked about *The Truman Show* is how I came to write it.

It is because I suspect it is true.

Who amongst us has not had the feeling that our friends, acquaintances, or even certain family members are acting? In my experience, many are *over*acting.

There are obvious giveaways. Occasionally an "extra" in your life—mailman, chiropractor, priest—will attempt to enlarge his role by launching into some melodramatic speech or in some other way try to upstage you.

And the continuity errors in this long-running production are there for all to see. The same background players and traffic keep cropping up over and over. You wander into a store on a whim and discover that the actors are not prepared for your arrival and know next to nothing about leather goods. You catch your best friend suddenly acting out of character or your mother dressed inappropriately. When confronted, these stars of your own particular situation-comedy are forced to hastily ad–lib but it is never very convincing.

Of course, throughout the show, hair and wardrobe are invariably a disaster—the first departments to feel any budget cuts. And the directing (*is* there a director?) is uneven at best.

However, my biggest criticism of the stage play people insist on calling "real life" is the script—varying between the mundanely predictable and the wildly implausible. Who writes this stuff?

INTRODUCTION

BY PETER WEIR

Andrew Niccol's screenplay deals with the last few days of a live television program which ran for twenty-nine years—twenty-four hours a day, seven days a week.

As part of my preparation I wrote a background describing how this extraordinary show came into existence. I had plenty of time for reflection as Jim Carrey wasn't available for twelve months, and believing him perfect casting as Truman I settled down to wait.

It seems impossible now that I considered doing another picture in the meantime, as the months filled up with constant rewrites and fine-tuning of the script.

Andrew and I worked well together and I felt free to try anything, in the process coming to know the material really well.

The background to the show I wrote for myself, but in preproduction cast and crew got to hear of it and asked for copies.

With the actors it became a source of amusement during shooting, particularly with Noah Emmerich, who played "Marlon," and Laura Linney as Truman's wife, "Meryl." We would ad-lib for hours, they in their actor persona (Marlon was "Louis Coltrane," Meryl, "Hannah Gill"), and with me playing, rather naturally, a director on the show. These ad-libs helped remind us of the schizophrenic nature of their characters, and kept us in touch with the lie that was at the heart of their relationship with Truman. Apart from that it was a lot of fun, and occasionally provoked ideas for new scenes.

I began to see potential for a documentary in these off-camera conversations and suggested the idea to the marketing department at Paramount. Andrew flew out to location and interviewed the cast in their actor personae and wrote a script we referred to as the "Mockumentary." My Visual Effects Supervisor and Second Unit Director, Mike McAlister, took on the job, with Harry Shearer as the interviewer.

The documentary was finally abandoned as a promotional idea but some scenes found their way into the movie and at least one version of the trailer.

Here then, with a little editing, is the background material passed on to cast and crew, which, in a way, serves as an introduction to Andrew's brilliant screenplay.

A SHORT HISTORY OF THE TRUMAN SHOW

Christof was twenty-nine years old when he sold his concept for what would become "The Truman Show" to multi-media giant, Omnicam.

His background was as a producer of documentaries, a field in which he had achieved considerable preeminence, winning an Academy Award for his deeply-moving record of street people—*Show Me the Way to Go Home*—when he was only twenty-three years old. For this program his director, Bob Lipski, lived on and off with a bunch of street kids for two years in a derelict building in Chicago. The kids themselves were unaware that the building was owned by Christof's uncle and had been pre-rigged with concealed cameras. The startling footage of life on the streets was graphic, hard-hitting, frankly sexual, and finally heart-wrenching. Christof and Lipski subsequently fell out, with Lipski bitterly charging Christof with taking all the credit for an idea he claimed he had submitted to Christof in the first place.

Earlier, while still a teenager, Christof edited his father's 8mm footage—a visual "diary" of Christof himself that his father had kept from an early age—into a film which did the film festival circuit. It was titled *A Life in the Day*, and at seven-and-three-quarter hours was described as either "brilliant" or "boring" by the critics. Christof arranged to have a debate with his detractors, which he then filmed and released as *The Artist at Bay*, which subsequently found a home on PBS.

So, only twenty-nine years old, this obsessive young man talked his way into the office of Moses Opperman, President and CEO of the world's largest media conglomerate, The Omnicam Corporation. Thirty minutes later he had the go-ahead for a program titled "Bringing Up Baby." The idea was to adopt a child, an unwanted pregnancy, and video, live, every moment of the child's life up to the age of one.

His parents were to be an attractive couple, actors, who would be involved in the extensive product placement that was to generate revenue for Omnicam. This was necessary as the show was to run twenty-four hours a day, every day, without commercial breaks.

The child was named "Truman" by Christof—"We will make of him a 'True Man'," Christof stated in a press-release at the time. As for "Burbank," that was where Truman's studio/home was to be located.

Christof, in a bold move, decided to open the show in the womb itself. Moses was concerned as there were, of course, extremely limited possibilities for product placement. However some companies, producing products for pregnant women, did place written messages on the show, which traveled across the image of the unborn child during peak viewing times.

From Truman's birth day onwards ratings began to steadily climb; by week 24 the show was a hit, and by week 36 a sensation. The reason was Truman. He was adorable and became "the world's baby." People even liked to watch him sleeping; it made them feel calm somehow, and the show became especially popular with seniors and childless couples, some even rigging up their television rooms like a nurseries, so they could tip-toe in to take a look at him on their TV set, making sure he was O.K., maybe closing the curtains to make it darker for his day sleep, before quietly leaving—the door left ajar so that they could hear him if he cried. A special "TV Crib" was marketed which enabled the TV set to be placed horizontal to the floor, so the viewer "parent" could look down on the sleeping child.

In the first weeks, the press made jokes—comparing the show to the burning log video, or saying it was like watching paint dry. But they had to write about it given the ratings, and in the end Truman won them over. He was a good-looking baby, with a calm, steady gaze from his big brown eyes, and with a wonderful chuckle. From an early age he liked to laugh. The slightest tickle produced deep rippling chuckles that put a smile on your face, and when the tears inevitably came, you felt tense until mom quieted him. down. And mom was the ideal mom. The good old apple-pie-mom of yesteryear—yet sexy too, in her own way, especially when she'd come in to give him his bottle in the middle of the night wearing a sheer, lowcut night-gown that showed off her curvaceous figure.

Costs were low in those early days—at first there was only the nursery set. Then, when ratings began to rise and sponsors of baby products clam-ored for their product to be used on the show, a kitchen was added. Then a garage for dad so his car could be featured, as well as all the tools in his workshop. Kirk was like a dad off the cover of *The Saturday Evening Post,* and Truman loved him. He always seemed closer to his dad for some reason—perhaps because dad was far and away the better actor.

A word about product placement on the show. If Truman played happily with, say, a "Snug-a-bug," that toy's sales broke records. But if he didn't like the "Wiggly-Twiggly" and threw it across the room in front of the mothers of the world, that company would inevitably have to withdraw the toy from the market. It was a risk placing a product on "The Truman Show," but the rewards could be staggering.

Christof, being the artist that he was, found the products an aggravation. But he couldn't do without them. He worked with the actors to show how to use the product with subtlety, so that it would seem a less obvious sell. And with the video-switchers in the control room, operating the concealed cameras (there was even one placed in the teat of Truman's bottle) Christof made sure they didn't dominate the frame with a Nappy Rash Pack or whatever product was being featured.

He wrote out storylines for the actors to keep the drama alive—low-key soap opera situations: tension at work for father, or mother talking about her period being late and how they couldn't afford another child. Just enough drama to make the viewer care about them and especially when the prob-lem threatened to include darling Truman.

Truman fan clubs sprang up worldwide, as did the beginning of what was to be a noisy opposition in later years, the "Free Truman Organization" and "Truth in Media." These two groups (later to combine as the TLF, the Truman Liberation Front) got as much press as possible to decry the exploitation of an innocent, etc. But there was no law against it, and Truman seemed very happy. Above all, a great deal of money was being made so nothing was done and the show became part of our lives.

During that first year the success of the show caused Moses to suggest to Christof that they extend for at least another year, taking Truman as far as his first spoken word, which Moses rightly guessed was going to be a ratings winner. (Already the show, at six months, was drawing a bigger audience than Omnicam's shopping channel).

Moses was puzzled when Christof laughed at his suggestion. "Why just another year, why not a lifetime?" (This historic sentence was engraved on a gold-plated bar by Moses and presented to Christof when the show became a phenomenon.)

What Christof proposed to Moses was unprecedented and staggering in its scope. He showed Moses plans for a new studio on a large parcel of land in Burbank, California. The studio was designed by ex-NASA scientists who had been working on a sealed environment for humans to live and work on Mars, a project that had been abandoned by a cash-strapped NASA.

This Bubble or Dome was to cover an entire town. Christof had the plans adapted for what he called Seahaven. Here we would watch Truman grow to manhood, facing all of the trials and tribulations we all face, but in a controlled environment. Thousands of concealed mini-cameras would be built into the "set" to cover every angle of the town, both exterior and interior.

This would be nothing less than a record of a human life from birth to death, every single moment live-to-air, and would create television history. Moses of course was thinking of the fantastic cost of the project balanced against the revenues that would result. Everything seen on the show would have a sponsor, the products available in a huge mail order catalogue. Christof hit Moses with figures that showed that within ten years costs could be recovered. In fact, they had their money back in five.

Moses was given a week to say yes or no, as Christof had a clause in his contract that enabled him to put young Truman into turnaround. Moses talked to his board the next morning and by lunchtime was on the company jet on his way to meet potential investors in Japan, Taiwan, (the show was very popular in Asia), Europe, and the Middle-East. He never flew beyond Tokyo. They wouldn't let him. The Japanese wanted to take all of the 49 percent Omnicam had on the table, and "The Truman Show" was born.

Christof's vision of Truman's world had its foundation in the past. "The future is the past," he was fond of saying, along with, "The way we were is the way we ought to be."

He despaired of the ugliness of modern urban life and saw a chance to inspire the world back to the small, close communities of nineteenth-century

America—the town square surrounded by neat clapboard houses, with front porches close to the street, white picket fences, few cars, all combining to form a cozy neighborhood where everyone knew everyone else and life was wholesome and simple. These homes were also for sale in kit form, and later many communities were constructed along the lines of Seahaven.

Clothing too came under his masterful eye. He felt that what people wore in the late 1930s and 1940s had approached an ideal, and his designers studied and produced an elegant line of clothing for the townsfolk, which proved another winner with the viewers.

Truman's education was planned carefully by Christof, and he exposed him to the best in art, literature, and music, but, ironically, very little television. Truman believed he was living in a remote part of Florida, where only one local television station was available, and it mostly played reruns of classic movies and television series such as "I Love Lucy." News was, of course, heavily censored and extolled the virtues of small town life compared with a dangerous, overcrowded, and troubled world.

Construction proceeded in stages. Truman was eighteen months old when he moved with his parents to a home in a quiet suburban street. For the next four years this was the only world he knew—his house, the backyard, the street, and the local park. And that was all the world there was at that time, while construction continued, beyond the sky cyclorama, on the city center, and Christof's boldest plan, the final stage: the beachfront and ocean. The technology involved in creating the ocean: wind, clouds, waves, etc., called on the top brains of the world. Moses argued in vain for an inland town, a sleepy rural community, but Christof, being the artist he was, refused to compromise—"It has to be real," was his continual cry.

Meanwhile, the world thrilled to Truman's first tooth, his first faltering steps, his first words. Then, his first day at school. Beyond that, there was facing down the school bully and his first exam and on to the stirrings of adolescence, teen rebellion, girls, etc.

Not that it was all drama, because apart from being a good-looking, sweet-natured boy, Truman was funny. He was a natural entertainer. He could make anyone laugh with his rubber face and his natural ability as a mimic. He was a star. People—even those with their own children—kept family snapshot albums of him and his family. Photos could be obtained, as well as custom photo albums, from the mail order catalogue. Kids of the same age or thereabouts saw him as a brother, experienced the same challenges as he did, at the same time he did. Truman became a real person to them, and he was a part of their lives.

In addition to the products available from the mail order department, Christof Enterprises produced board games, swap cards, etc. The biggest seller was Truman Trivia, a board game which posed questions about the minutiae of Truman's life.

Articles and books on the subject of the show, came from all sources. There were scientific articles about the technology involved in creating the studio (NASA reactivated their plans for a Space City on Mars, incorporating ideas developed by Christof's team). Then, of course, sociologists, psychiatrists, and assorted medicos wrote articles and books pro and con the extraordinary experiment. Actors signed book deals—*Living A Part, Live, With Truman, The Method and the Truman Show,* etc.

So much was the show discussed by television viewers of the world that major English dictionaries accepted a new word that had become part of the vernacular:

> **Tru·man·esque** (—esk'), *adj.* a characteristic of the life experiences of Truman Burbank *(a Trumanesque town, conversation, etc.)*

Meanwhile, Truman lived on, unaware that his life was unlike any other. After all, why should he doubt his world? It was all he'd ever known and as real to him as ours is to us. (It was regrettable that Christof was forced to make him a fearful boy. He was too adventurous, and there was a danger of him discovering the limit of his world.)

For some of the key actors, those required to live on the set full-time, life on the show did become, in a sense, a reality. The line between truth and fiction was blurred. Not that just any actor could take that life. Potential cast members didn't just audition in the usual way, they had to pass tests every bit as rigorous as would those eventually sent to artificial environments on other planets.

Christof's reputation as a new kind of producer—a videographer— soared with the ratings of the show and he became an international celebrity. Not that he was seen about much, except at the Emmys (the "Show" frequently a nominee or winner) as he lived a hermitic existence at the studio, where he had an apartment down the corridor from the control room. To say he was obsessed with the show would be an understatement. Like Truman, he lived most of these years inside the world he'd created, until it became for him the only world.

He was something of a hypochondriac and the only reason he wouldn't be at the studio was that he was having his blood replaced at a health farm in Switzerland, or in the hospital with nervous exhaustion, or, of course, visiting his shrink. This renowned doctor, with Christof's permission, later wrote a remarkable book, *The Creator*.

There were highs and lows in the ratings over the years, the show going through a rather bad slump in the later years prior to Truman's departure. Would it have gone with Truman to the grave? Nobody knows, nor will they ever know, as it's unlikely there'll be another Truman, as witnessed by countless "reality" shows that attempted to emulate the success of "The Truman Show" and failed.

Extract from the *Guinness Book of Records:*

> "...while the longest-running, continuous, (24 hours a day, 7 days a week) live television program in history was "The Truman Show." The program was broadcast from a single studio in Burbank, California (SEE Largest Inflatable Structure in the world, p. 987) and sent live to the world via satellite by U.S. broadcast giant, The Omnicam Corporation. The show, which occupied its own channel, ran for twenty-nine years, ending when the star, Truman Burbank, an orphan unaware that the town in which he lived was a stage-set or that his every move had been filmed from birth, discovered the "secret" and walked away from the show (SEE Most Watched Television Events, p. 549).

Subsequent legislation in the United States has prevented any further exploitation of this kind, although similar programs have since been attempted from countries with lax media laws. So far no show has proved to have the staying power of "The Truman Show."

---

* *The Creator—Stress and the God-Complex in Corporate America,* by Karl Otto Wurdig, M.D. Publisher: Omnicam Corp., New York, NY.

THE SHOOTING SCRIPT™

THE TRUMAN SHOW

THE TRUMAN SHOW

An Original Screenplay

by

Andrew Niccol

Shooting Script

A FOGGED MIRROR

Behind the fog we hear the sounds of a bathroom. After a
long moment, a hand wipes the condensation from the glass to
reveal the face of TRUMAN BURBANK. He wears a sleeveless
Hanes undershirt and blue-stripe pajama bottoms, behind him a
white glazed tiled bathroom wall. It is immediately apparent
that we are viewing him through a two-way mirror.

Truman, expressionless, studies his reflection in the mirror.
For a long moment, he does nothing. He continues to look
impassively into the mirror for what becomes an uncomfortably
long time. Still nothing. Finally he speaks, talking to
himself in the mirror as if participating in a TV interview.

> TRUMAN
> ...personally I think the unconquered
> south face is the only one worth
> scaling...of course it's a 20,000 foot
> sheer wall of ice but then when did that
> ever stop me before?...Naturally, I
> intend to make the ascent without the
> benefit of oxygen but also without
> crampons or even an ice pick...*risks?*...
>> (smug, TV smile)
> ...sure I'm aware of the risks--why else
> do you think I would spend seven years as
> an adjuster in a life insurance
> company...?

> MERYL (O.S.)
> Truman, you're gonna be late!

Truman resignedly opens the door of the cabinet and replaces
his shaving tackle. It partially obscures the lens of the
hidden camera. He closes the door and exits.

INT. KITCHEN. MORNING.

MERYL, wearing a stylish robe, sits at the kitchen table
sipping coffee. On the table in front of her lies a parcel.
TRUMAN enters and glances at the gift.

> TRUMAN
> What's that?

> MERYL
> It's a surprise.

TRUMAN unwraps the parcel - an expensive-looking set of
exercise sweats.

>   MERYL
>   (eager for his response)
>   Well, what do you think?

>   TRUMAN
>   They're...
>   (the merest hesitation)
>   perfect. Thank you.

Truman returns Meryl's kiss.

>   MERYL
>   (handing him the sweat top)
>   Try it on.

Truman pulls the top over his head. As he does so, a closer
shot focuses on the manufacturer's name.

>   MERYL
>   I thought you could wear them when you do
>   your exercises.
>   (afterthought)
>   Pre-shrunk. And they breathe.

3   EXT. TRUMAN'S HOUSE. DAY.   3

Wearing a business suit, briefcase in hand, TRUMAN emerges
from his pleasant, Victorian-inspired, picket-fenced house
into an idyllic suburban street of similarly picturesque
homes. A neighbor, SPENCER, is taking in trashcans,
whistling a tune. Spencer breaks off abruptly as Truman
approaches his car. His license plate reads, *Seahaven - A
Nice Place To Live*".

>   SPENCER
>   Morning, Truman.

>   TRUMAN
>   Morning, Spencer. And in case I don't
>   see you, good afternoon, good evening
>   and good night.

Spencer's dog, PLUTO, bounds happily over to Truman.

>   TRUMAN
>   (petting the dog)
>   Hey, Pluto.

Truman exchanges a polite nod with the WASHINGTON's, an
African-American family across the street. MR. WASHINGTON
is farewelled by his WIFE and CHILD.

3   CONTINUED: 3

Truman is about to climb into his car when he is distracted
by a high-pitched whistling sound. Suddenly, a large
spherical glass object falls from the sky and lands with a
deafening crash on the street, several yards from his car.

         rtled Truman looks to Spencer but he has abruptly
         ared inside his house with Pluto. Mrs. Washington and
Washington Junior have also made themselves scarce.

Truman investigates. Amidst a sea of shattered glass are the
remains of a light mechanism.

He looks around him but the street is deserted. He checks
that all the surrounding street lights are accounted for,
even though the fallen fixture is far larger. He looks up
into the sky but there is no plane in sight. With some
effort, Truman picks up what's left of the crumpled light and
loads it into the trunk. A label on the light fixture reads,
"SIRIUS (9 Canis Major)". As he drives away, we hear the
sound of his car radio.

                    RADIO ANNOUNCER
              Another glorious morning in Seahaven,
              folks.

3A   INT./EXT.   TRUMAN'S CAR - SEAHAVEN. DAY.   3A

TRUMAN makes his way along the streets of Seahaven past a
series of quaint, pastel-shaded cottages.

4   EXT.   SEAHAVEN ISLAND TOWNSHIP. DAY.   4

A high-angle reveals an anonymous mid-sized town built around
a small, pretty bay. A cluster of high-rise buildings stand
at the water's edge overlooking a marina. Surrounding the
commercial center lie neatly arranged suburbs.

5   EXT.   OCEANSIDE STREET. DAY.   5

Pausing at a traffic light along a seaside road, TRUMAN looks
through a curious wooden arch to the beach and ocean beyond.
The sight triggers a memory in his head.

6   PLAYBACK - EXT. LONG, WIDE BEACH. DAY.   6

Unlike a conventional flashback, the scene in his memory
appears to be playing on a television screen.

(CONTINUED)

6   CONTINUED: 6

FOUR-YEAR-OLD TRUMAN runs towards a bluff on the beach.

The boy's father, KIRK, late-thirties, beer bottle in hand,
flirts with TWO TEENAGE GIRLS at the shoreline. Suddenly,
the father remembers his son. He looks anxiously around.
The sight of the boy at the far end of the beach causes him
to drop his bottle in the sand and run to Truman.

The boy is near the top of the cliff before his agitated
father comes within earshot.

                    FATHER
            (out of breath, clutching his side)
        Truman! Truman! Stop!

Truman turns from his perch and waves happily down to his
father. But the smile quickly vanishes when he registers the
anger and distress on his father's face.

                    FATHER
        Come down now!

His father's unnatural anxiety makes the next bay even more
tantalizing. The boy considers defying his father. He puts
his hand on the rock above him to stretch up and sneak a peek
at the other side. One good stretch would do it.

                    FATHER
            (reading Truman's mind, enraged)
        No!

                    TRUMAN
        Why? What's there?

                    FATHER
            (unconvincing)
        Nothing. It's...it's dangerous.
            (trace of desperation)
        Come down, now! Please!

Truman is suddenly aware that the hundreds of other
BEACHGOERS have stopped their activities to stare at him.
Reluctantly, he starts to retrace his steps down the rocks.
When he finally jumps to the sand, his father embraces him
and leads him away.

                    FATHER
        I told you to stay close. Don't ever
        leave my sight again.
            (pause)
        You've got to know your limitations. You
        could've fallen.

7   INT.   TRUMAN'S CAR - DOWNTOWN SEAHAVEN.   MORNING - *PRESENT*.   7

Through his car window, TRUMAN buys a cup of coffee from a
streetside VENDOR.

                        VENDOR
              How are ya, Truman?

                        TRUMAN
                 (placing his fingers to his pulse)
              Vital signs are good.

He pulls into a parking space and sips on the coffee. As he
drinks, he becomes aware of a school bell summoning children
to class in the adjacent Elementary School. The image
prompts another childhood memory.

8   *PLAYBACK* - INT.   SEAHAVEN ELEMENTARY SCHOOL - CLASSROOM.   DAY.   8

*Once again, the flashback appears to be playing on a
television screen.*

SEVEN-YEAR-OLD TRUMAN sits in the middle row of an Elementary
School classroom surrounded by twenty-or-so other well-
scrubbed, uniformed YOUNGSTERS.   MARLON, the boy next to
Truman, is on his feet under the scrutiny of a kindly Norman
Rockwell-style SCHOOL MISTRESS.

                        SCHOOL MISTRESS
              What do you want to do when you grow up,
              Marlon?

                        MARLON
              I want to be an entrepreneur like my dad.

                        SCHOOL MISTRESS
                 (impressed)
              Tell the class what an "entrepreneur"
              does, Marlon.

                        MARLON
              He makes a lot of money, Ma'am.

                        SCHOOL MISTRESS
              A good one does, Marlon.
                 (looking in her purse,
                 hamming it up)
              Perhaps I'll be coming to you for a loan
              one of these days.

The CLASS titters. Marlon sits down and winks to Truman.

                                                          (CONTINUED)

8   CONTINUED: 8

                        SCHOOL MISTRESS
               What about you, Truman?

Truman rises to his feet, gathering his nerve.

                        TRUMAN
               I want to be an explorer
                    (with reverence)
               ...like *Magellan.*

The School Mistress smiles benevolently.

                        SCHOOL MISTRESS
                    (slightly condescending)
               I'm afraid no one's going to pay you to
               do that, Truman. You might have to find
               something a little more practical.
                    (glancing to a pulldown wall
                    map behind her head)
               Besides, you're too late. There's really
               nothing left to explore.

The class roars with laughter as the crestfallen Truman takes
his seat.

9   EXT. PARKING LOT. DAY - *PRESENT.*   9

TRUMAN, briefcase in hand, crosses from the parking lot to
the town square, surrounded by similarly suited, briefcase-
toting OFFICE WORKERS.

10   EXT. DOWNTOWN SEAHAVEN. DAY.   10

TRUMAN walks briskly down the bustling city street. A snarl
of taxis, buses and COMMUTER traffic. A STREET VENDOR
thrusts a pretzel under Truman's nose, a CAREER WOMAN tries
to catch his eye.

Truman stops at a kiosk and buys a newspaper - *"THE ISLAND TIMES"*.

                        VENDOR
               Is that all for you, Truman?

                        TRUMAN
               That's all. Thanks, Errol.

Other CUSTOMERS also purchase the morning paper. Tucking his
copy under his arm, Truman selects a glossy magazine from a
rack, quickly flicking through the pages.

                                                          (CONTINUED)

10   CONTINUED: 10

Glancing in the direction of the NEWSPAPER VENDOR and finding
him busy with another CUSTOMER, Truman deftly tears a portion
of the open page and pockets the cutting. He hastily
replaces the magazine and departs.

As Truman hurries away, the Vendor exits the kiosk and picks
up the magazine, instantly turning to the torn page. It is a
cosmetics advertisement with the MODEL'S NOSE missing.
However, the Vendor makes no effort to confront Truman,
almost as if he were expecting it.

11   EXT. SEAHAVEN LIFE AND ACCIDENT, INC. DAY.   11

Truman passes along a row of shops and offices, finally
entering a building that proudly proclaims, *"Seahaven Life &
Accident Inc."* above the entrance. He has evidently taken
his teacher's advice.

12   INT. INSURANCE COMPANY - SEAHAVEN LIFE AND ACCIDENT, INC. DAY.   12

In a cramped, cluttered cubicle, TRUMAN talks on the telephone.

                    TRUMAN
               (into receiver)
          ...okay, okay, let's call it what it
          is... I'm not going to lie to you...life
          insurance is death insurance...you've
          just got to ask yourself two questions...
          one, in the event of your death, will
          anyone experience financial loss?...and
          two, do you care?

A CLERK drops a large reference book on Truman's desk.
Truman checks the spine - *"MARITIME ACCIDENTS"*.

                    TRUMAN
               (into receiver)
          Hold on will you?
               (to Clerk, referring to the book)
          This is no good. Lumps all maritime
          accidents together. I need drownings as
          a separate category.

The Clerk shrugs, returns the book to his cart and continues
his rounds.

                    TRUMAN
               (returning to his call)
          ...just think about what I've been saying
          and let me...hello?...

                                              (CONTINUED)

The person on the other end has hung up. With an apathetic shrug, Truman replaces the receiver. He looks over his shoulder and places another call.

>   TRUMAN
>   (lowering his voice)
>   Can you connect me with directory
>   inquiries in Fiji?

A CO-WORKER suddenly pokes his head over the neigboring cubicle.

>   CO-WORKER
>   What do you know, Truman?

>   TRUMAN
>   (embarrassed, mouthing the word)
>   --Can't talk.
>   (waving off his neighbor, pretending
>   to be on a business call)
>   I'm sorry, Ma'am. If he's in a coma,
>   he's probably uninsurable.

The Co-Worker disappears back into his own cubicle.

>   TRUMAN
>   (lowering his voice again)
>   Hello, operator...yes, *Fiji*...Do you have
>   a listing for a Lauren Garland...?
>   (pause)
>   ...nothing listed?...what about a *Sylvia*
>   Garland..."S" for Sylvia...nothing?
>   Okay, thanks...

The disconsolate Truman replaces the receiver. Other INSURANCE AGENTS are heading to lunch. Truman puts on his jacket and follows them to the elevators.

13   INT. LOCAL ITALIAN DELI. LUNCHTIME.   13

Behind a deli counter, TYRONE, fifties, is having his hair brushed by a YOUNGER MAN. The man fusses one final time then swiftly departs through a rear door just as TRUMAN enters the store. Tyrone has anticipated Truman's order and has already begun preparing a meatball and mozzarella sandwich on an Italian roll. Truman gazes at the sandwich skillfully under construction, pained by his own predictability.

>   TYRONE
>   (nauseatingly cheerful)
>   How's it going, Truman?

13   CONTINUED: 13

                         TRUMAN
                     (deadpan)
            Not bad. I just won the State Lottery.

                         TYRONE
                     (not listening to Truman's reply)
            Good. Good.

                         TRUMAN
            Tyrone, what if I said I didn't want
            meatball today?

                         TYRONE
                     (not missing a beat, passing
                     Truman his wrapped sandwich)
            I'd ask for identification.

      Truman forces a half-smile and exits.

                         TYRONE
            See you tomorrow, Truman.

                         TRUMAN
            You can count on it.

14   EXT. SECLUDED PARK. DAY.   14

      TRUMAN eats lunch alone at a small, out-of-the-way park
      dominated by a gazebo. From his briefcase he pulls out an
      old, hardcovered book, *To The Ends Of The Earth - The Age Of
      Exploration*. He reads to himself, his sandwich uneaten
      beside him. Struck by a particular passage, he reads aloud.

                         TRUMAN
            "With a mutiny but half-repressed and
            starvation imminent, he pressed southward
            till he found the long-hoped-for
            straits..."

      Truman is interrupted by a TRANSIENT in a wheelchair. It is
      the man's sneakers Truman notices first, over the top of his
      book - they are distinctively initialed, "T.S.". Still under
      the spell of the account of Magellan, he hands the grateful
      man his sandwich.

15   INT. A CONFERENCE ROOM SOMEWHERE. DAY.   15

      A group of a dozen MEN and WOMEN of varying ages sit around a
      circular conference table in a sterile, windowless meeting room.
      All stare at a single telephone placed in the center of the
      table, anticipating a call. On cue, the phone rings and one of
      the men, after waiting for the second ring, picks up.

                                                        (CONTINUED)

15   CONTINUED: 15

                              MAN
                    Hello?...I'm sorry, I've got more than
                    enough life insurance.

He hangs up. After a moment the phone rings again.

16   INT. INSURANCE COMPANY. DAY.   16

TRUMAN sits at his desk, making a cold call.

                              TRUMAN
                         (into receiver)
                    ...this isn't about insurance, this is
                    about the great variable - when will
                    death occur? Could be a week, a month, a
                    year. Could happen today...A sunbather,
                    minding his own business, gets stabbed in
                    the heart by the tip of a runaway beach
                    umbrella... No way you can guard against
                    that kind of thing, no way at all...

The prospect on the other end, unimpressed with Truman's
pitch, hangs up. Truman's supervisor, LAWRENCE, younger than
Truman by several years, sharper suit, sharper haircut,
appears around the corner of the cubicle.

                              LAWRENCE
                         (handing Truman some
                         documentation)
                    Hey, Burbank, I've got a prospect in
                    Welles Park I need you to close.

Truman's face falls. He stares out of his third floor window
at the hazy skyline of a nearby island across the bay.

                              TRUMAN
                         (referring to the island)
                    Welles Park on Harbor Island?

                              LAWRENCE
                         (sarcastic)
                    You know another one?

                              TRUMAN
                    I can't do it.
                         (searching for a plausible
                         excuse)
                    --I've got an appointment--er, dentist.

(CONTINUED)

16   CONTINUED: 16

                         LAWRENCE
                    (insistent)
               You'll lose a lot more than your teeth if
               you don't meet your quota, Burbank.
                    (the threat in his voice is
                     unmistakable)
               They're making cutbacks at the end of the
               month. You need this.
                    (as he exits the cubicle)
               Besides, a half hour across the bay. Sea
               air. Do you good.

          Truman sinks back into his seat and stares out at the distant
          skyline. The buildings appear very still. Truman picks up a
          photo of his wife, Meryl, deposits it in his briefcase and
          exits.

16A   EXT. SEAHAVEN. DAY.   16A

          Truman's car heads out of the city on its way to the ferry.

17   INT. SEAHAVEN FERRY TERMINAL. DAY.   17

          TRUMAN exits his car. Mustering all his nerve, he marches
          into the Seahaven terminal and buys a token for the ferry.

          Out of his hearing, TWO FERRY WORKERS observe Truman's
          agitated behavior.

                         FERRY WORKER 1
               I got a feeling this is the day.

                         FERRY WORKER 2
               No way. I say he makes it through the
               turnstiles but he never gets on.

          The two men shake on the wager. Unaware of the scrutiny,
          Truman passes through the turnstiles with a herd of TOURISTS
          and COMMUTERS. He makes his way across the terminal, but
          abruptly pulls up at the gangway.

          As the other PASSENGERS impatiently brush past him onto the
          boat, Truman remains frozen to the spot, mesmerized by the
          scummy water rising and falling beneath the dock. It
          triggers a memory in his head.

18   *PLAYBACK* - EXT. SEAHAVEN HARBOR. DUSK.   18

          As always, the flashback appears to play on a television
          screen.

                                                            (CONTINUED)

18   CONTINUED: 18

SEVEN-YEAR-OLD TRUMAN, wearing a lifejacket, sits alongside
his father, KIRK, in a small sailing dinghy, sailing into a
stiff breeze.

A second sail boat circles them. We observe the father and
son from an angle atop the mast of the neighboring vessel.

                    TRUMAN
              (shouting above the wind)
         Let's go further, daddy! Let's go
         further!

                    KIRK
              (shouting back)
         It's getting rough, Truman.

                    TRUMAN
              (entreating his father)
         Please!...

Kirk shakes his head ruefully and indulges his son by heading
towards the gathering storm clouds on the horizon.

19   INT. SEAHAVEN FERRY TERMINAL. DAY - *PRESENT*.   19

Truman turns and begins to fight his way back against the tide of
PASSENGERS boarding the ferry, emerging back onto the street,
gasping for air. The FERRY WORKERS settle their wager.

20   EXT. ROADWAY ADJACENT TO THE FERRY TERMINAL. DAY.   20

TRUMAN stands at a payphone. By stretching the payphone's
receiver cord as far as it will go, he is just able to reach
his arm and leg into the driver's door of his car. He
punctuates his conversation with blasts on the car's horn
while revving the car's engine with his outstretched foot.
The few passing MOTORISTS and PEDESTRIANS regard Truman
curiously.

                    TRUMAN
              (shouting into phone)
         --I tell you the traffic's insane.
              (blasting his horn several
              times to imitate the sound of
              gridlock)
         ...I'll never make the ferry in time.
         What can I do?--*what?*...Lawrence, I can't
         hear you!

Truman hangs up the phone.

21   INT. TRUMAN'S CAR. DAY.   21

On his way home, a large *"DETOUR"* sign forces him onto a
secondary road.

22   INT. TRUMAN'S CAR - PARKLAND, SEAHAVEN. DAY.   22

TRUMAN drives along a winding road through parkland. He
pulls up at a red light - no other traffic around. His
attention is caught by an attractive YOUNG WOMAN, sitting on
a park bench not far from the intersection. She is being
taunted by TWO YOUNG THUGS. She attempts to ignore the
youths by concentrating on the book on her lap.

                    YOUTH 1
                 (to woman)
              You wanna read to me?

His companion smirks.

                    YOUTH 1
                 (more insistent)
              You wanna read to me?

The boy reaches over and snatches the novel from her grasp.

                    YOUTH 2
                 (menacing)
              My friend asked you a question.

The woman picks up her bag in a reflex and holds it to her.
She looks about for assistance, briefly catching Truman's eye.
The youths also look in Truman's direction, staring him down.

                    WOMAN
                 (reaching for the book)
              Please...

The boy returns the book to the woman, but before doing so
rips out the last page from the novel and stuffs it in his
shirt pocket.

                    YOUTH 2
              Now you're gonna have to ask me how
              it ends.

One of the youths grabs the woman, dragging her toward the
surrounding woods.

                    YOUTH 1
              We're gonna tell you how it ends, baby.

                                              (CONTINUED)

22   CONTINUED: 22

                              WOMAN
                    Help! Please help!

As they drag her towards the undergrowth, Truman, horrified,
half gets out of the car - fearful of his own safety as much
as the woman's. Truman shouts to the youths, his voice
cracking with fear.

                              TRUMAN
                    Hey! Let her go!

A huge truck suddenly appears behind Truman's car, its horn
blasting, the DRIVER hurling abuse. Truman hesitates as the
youths drag the woman into the bushes, conflicted over
whether or not to help. The truck driver keeps his hand on
the horn. Truman retreats back into his car and reluctantly
drives on.

23   EXT. PARKLAND - WOODS. DAY.   23

Truman's car safely out of sight, the YOUTHS promptly release
the YOUNG WOMAN. She calmly brushes herself off, no longer
afraid. The young men, no longer angry, retrieve her bag.

                              WOMAN
                    Thanks.

The threesome walks back towards the roadway as if life-long
friends.

                              WOMAN
                    (pondering the incident)
                    He did nothing.

                              YOUTH 1
                    (shrugs, suddenly more couth)
                    Physical violence paralyzes him. Always has.

24   EXT. TRUMAN'S HOUSE. DUSK.   24

Beyond the pretty picket fence at the end of the property
flows a busy highway.

TRUMAN is mowing the lawn. From his expression it would seem
that he's still reflecting on his inaction in the park. He
switches off the mower and leans on the handle.

He is distracted by the arrival of his wife, MERYL, exiting
the house. She wears a nurse's uniform and carries a curious
metal device attached to a cardboard backing. She kisses
Truman affectionately on the cheek.

                                                      (CONTINUED)

24   CONTINUED: 24

                              MERYL
              Hi, honey. Look at this.
                   (proudly referring to the device)
              It's a "Chef's-Mate". Dicer, slicer and
              peeler in one. Never needs sharpening.
              Dishwasher safe.

                              TRUMAN
              Gee, that's great.

Looking over Truman's shoulder, Meryl notices a small, uncut
patch of grass missed by Truman in one of his passes.

                              MERYL
                   (referring to the uncut grass)
              You missed a section.

Meryl enters the house. Truman restarts the lawnmower and
obediently pushes it towards the offending patch of lawn. As
the mower brushes up against the unconforming blades of
grass, Truman pulls back abruptly. He checks the kitchen
window for Meryl and wheels the mower away, leaving the patch
uncut.

25   INT. TRUMAN'S HOUSE - LIVING ROOM. NIGHT.   25

MERYL is removing the cap of her nurse's uniform when TRUMAN
enters.

                              TRUMAN
              How did it go today?

                              MERYL
                   (matter-of-fact)
              A man tripped and fell on a chainsaw.
                   (shrug)
              We got three of his fingers back on.

Truman retrieves a bucket of golf balls and a golf club from
behind the door.

                              MERYL
                   (disappointed at the sight of
                    the golf equipment)
              I was hoping we could have a special
              evening.

                              TRUMAN
              I won't be late.

                                                              (CONTINUED)

25   CONTINUED: 25

                              MERYL
                        (sensing something odd in his
                        demeanor)
                   Did something happen today?

Truman turns to her too sharply, his guilt showing.

                              TRUMAN
                   What could happen?

Truman exits.

26   EXT. UNFINISHED BRIDGE. NIGHT.   26

A half-constructed bridge, paved but unmarked, ends abruptly
in mid-air - reinforcing steel protruding from the concrete.
TRUMAN stands at the end of the unfinished bridge with
MARLON, thirties, a well-filled physique. Marlon drinks beer
from a can while Truman addresses a teed-up golf ball with a
number three wood. The headlights of their two parked cars
light the cement "fairway". Their target is a sign at the
far end of the bridge proclaiming, *"THE SEAHAVEN CAUSEWAY -
Linking Seahaven Island With The Rest Of The World - Your Tax
Dollars At Work"* - an upturned plastic cone at the foot of
the sign is the "hole".

Truman winds up and swings, making healthy contact with the
ball. The ball arches away into the night sky. From a new
angle we see the ball take a huge hop on the outside lane of
the abandoned freeway and continue down the asphalt beyond
the sign.

Marlon tosses Truman another off-white ball from a bucket of
badly scarred golf balls. Truman sets the ball up on the
makeshift tee area and launches himself into his second shot.
With a slight fade, the second ball carries even further than
the first.

                              MARLON
                   Whose nuts were those?

Truman hands Marlon their sole golf club without comment.
Marlon tees up a ball of his own. He uses orange golf balls.

                              TRUMAN
                   I'm thinking of getting out, Marlon.

                              MARLON
                        (mild interest only)
                   Yeah? Outta what?

> TRUMAN
> Outta my job, outta Seahaven, off this
> island...*out!*

Marlon takes a practice swing.

> MARLON
> Outta your job? What the hell's wrong
> with your job? You gotta great job. You
> gotta desk job. I'd kill for a desk job.

Marlon addresses the ball and swings - a sweeping hook shot
that bounces off the freeway and into the water hazard.

> MARLON
> (annoyed by the errant tee shot)
> Sonofabitch.
> (still looking in the
> direction of his ball)
> Try stocking vending machines for a
> living. My biggest decision of the day
> is whether the Almond Joys look better
> next to the Snickers or the Baby Ruths.

Truman selects another "M" ball from the bucket and tosses it
to Marlon.

> TRUMAN
> (adamant)
> Haven't you ever gotten itchy feet?

Overcompensating with his second shot, Marlon slices the ball in
the other direction. A lucky bounce keeps it on the "green".
The ball rolls in the direction of the upturned cone.

> MARLON
> (skeptical, picking up his beer)
> Where is there to go?

Truman gulps his beer as he prepares his answer.

> TRUMAN
> (unable to disguise his
> reverence)
> *Fiji.*

Marlon considers Truman's suggestion as he sips his beer.

> MARLON
> (impressed)
> Fiji? Where the hell is Fiji exactly?
> Near Florida? You can't drive there,
> can you?

(CONTINUED)

26   CONTINUED: (2)   26

Truman picks up a golf ball to demonstrate. He points to a
dimple on his make-shift globe.

                    TRUMAN
          See here, this is us.
                    (sliding his finger around
                    the other side of the ball)
          All the way round here, Fiji. You can't
          get any further away before you start
          coming back.
                    (tossing the world in his
                    hand, warming to his subject)
          Y'know, there are still islands in Fiji
          where no human being has ever set foot.

                    MARLON
                    (still dubious)
          So when are you leaving?

                    TRUMAN
          It's not that simple. Takes money,
          planning. You can't just up and go.
                    (heading off Marlon's skepticism)
          Oh, I'm going to do it, don't worry about
          that. I've just got to move slow. Pick
          my moment. Bonus time's just around the
          corner. Soon as I finish the...

                    MARLON
          Nursery?

                    TRUMAN
          Spare room -- I can start thinking about
          selling up...and I'll be gone. Up and
          away on that big steel bird.
                    (as if to convince himself)
          I'm going, don't you worry about that.

Marlon nods even though the concept of taking flight is
beyond his imagination.

                    MARLON
          I never knew anybody who wanted to leave
          Seahaven.

An awkward moment. Truman, once again, not so sure of himself.

27   INT. A DIMLY-LIT ROOM SOMEWHERE. NIGHT.   27

A MAN looks up sharply. He stares into camera. CHRISTOF, late
fifties - a vitality in his eyes that belies his years. A news
anchor-style earpiece disappears down the neck of his suit.

28   EXT. BRIDGE. NIGHT.   28

TRUMAN and MARLON wander along the empty bridge, retrieving
the golf balls.

Marlon goes to say something to the disconsolate Truman, but
is momentarily distracted. He raises his hand to his ear.
Truman places another of the balls in the bucket.

                    MARLON
               Truman, you know, I did think about
               moving away one time.

                    TRUMAN
                    (interest piqued)
               Yeah, what happened?

                    MARLON
               I figured, what's the point? I knew I'd
               just be taking my problems with me. Once
               the kids came along, it made me look at
               Seahaven with new eyes.
                    (gazing out at the lights of
                     Seahaven)
               I realized, what the hell could be better
               than this?
                    (putting a hand on Truman's
                     shoulder)
               I'm telling you. What you really need is
               someone to carry on the "Burbank" name.

                    TRUMAN
               You think so?

                    MARLON
               Trust me.

Marlon picks up the last ball at the mouth of the upturned
cone. The ball is white.

                    MARLON
                    (checking the ball)
               You win.

They approach Truman's car. Truman opens the trunk to
deposit their humble golfing equipment. Inside are the
remains of the fallen light fixture.

                    TRUMAN
                    (referring to the light)
               You really think it could've dropped off
               an airliner?

(CONTINUED)

28   CONTINUED: 28

                         MARLON
                       (unimpressed)
               Sure. It's halogen. Shame it didn't hit
               you - you could've sued.
                       (quickly changing the subject)
               You coming for a drink?

                         TRUMAN
               I can't tonight.

29   INT. LIGHTHOUSE. NIGHT.   29

      From the POV of the lighthouse's lantern room, we observe
      TRUMAN sitting on the beach staring out to sea.

      Closer on Truman. He has a portable tape recorder slung over
      his shoulder and points a corded microphone at the surf. We
      watch Truman's impassive face as he makes the recording of
      the lapping waves. The lamp from the lighthouse occasionally
      falls upon Truman.

30   *PLAYBACK - EXT. OCEAN. DAY.*   30

      As always, the flashback appears to play on a television screen.

      The sky is black with storm clouds. Gale force winds lash
      rain into the faces of SEVEN-YEAR-OLD TRUMAN and his father,
      KIRK. As Kirk stands up to get his bearings, a freak gust of
      wind catches the sail. The boom whips across the stern and
      strikes Kirk flush in the head, knocking him overboard.

      Truman, wearing the sole lifejacket, desperately reaches for
      his father. He momentarily has hold of his father's hand
      when Kirk is abruptly dragged beneath the surface.

                         TRUMAN
                       (crying out)
               Daddy!!...Daddy!!...

      His cries go unanswered. Seven-year-old Truman finds himself
      alone - the storm abruptly passed, the wind suddenly dropped,
      the water stilled.

      The frightened Truman examines the ring he holds in his open
      hand - his father's ring - wrenched from his finger in
      Truman's fight to keep him afloat.

31   EXT. BEACH. NIGHT - *PRESENT*.   31

A close up of TRUMAN from KIRK'S RING that Truman now wears.

Then, from the lighthouse POV, we observe Truman get to his
feet and walk towards the dark water. He stands at the
water's edge.

                    TRUMAN
              (shouting at the surf)
         I'm sorry, Dad! I'm sorry!

As if in reply, a tongue of lightning flashes across the
distant skyline, followed by a growl of thunder.

32   INT. A LIVING ROOM SOMEWHERE. NIGHT.   32

TWO OLD WOMEN, seventies, sit beside each other on a sofa
looking directly into camera as they talk.

                    OLD WOMAN 1
              (playing amateur psychiatrist)
         It left him with more than his obvious
         fear of the water.

                    OLD WOMAN 2
         He was never the same curious little
         boy again.

                    OLD WOMAN 1
         Half the women I know named their
         children after him.

33   EXT. BEACH PARKING LOT. NIGHT.   33

TRUMAN is forced to leg it through a sudden rain shower to
his car.

From Truman's point-of-view, the shower appears quite normal.
However, viewed from a distance, we see that the shower is
extremely localized, encircling only him, as if a small cloud
is directly above his head, tracking his progress.

As Truman crosses the parking lot, the shower crosses with
him. Sensing something amiss, Truman dances back and forth
across the street, intrigued by the curious phenomenon. He
hums a few bars of "Singin' In The Rain".

The rain becomes heavier, covering a wider area. Truman runs
the remaining distance to his car.

34   INT.   TRUMAN'S HOUSE - NURSERY. NIGHT.   34

The drenched TRUMAN enters to find MERYL in the unfinished
nursery, comparing wallpaper samples. Meryl wears a robe, a
glimpse of black negligee beneath.

                    MERYL
          Where have you been?

                    TRUMAN
               (wringing out his jacket)
          I've been thinking--

                    MERYL
               (rolling her eyes)
          Oh, God.

                    TRUMAN
               (ignoring the reaction)
          --I figure we could scrape together
          eight thousand.

                    MERYL
               (exasperated)
          Every time you and Marlon--

                    TRUMAN
          --We could bum around the world for a
          year on that.

                    MERYL
          And then what, Truman? We'd be back to
          where we were five years ago. You're
          talking like a teenager.

                    TRUMAN
          Maybe I feel like a teenager.

                    MERYL
          We're mortgaged to the eyeballs, Truman.
          There's the car payments. Are we just
          going to walk away from our financial
          obligations?

Truman, still dripping on the floor, holds Meryl by the arms.
He talks excitedly to her the way we imagine he did when they
were courting.

                    TRUMAN
          It'd be an adventure.

                                              (CONTINUED)

34   CONTINUED: 34

                         MERYL
               I thought we were going to try for a
               baby. Isn't that enough of an adventure?

                         TRUMAN
               That can wait. I want to get away. See
               some of the world. Explore.

Meryl gives a derisive laugh.

                         MERYL
               You want to be an explorer? You don't
               even have a passport, Truman. I bet you
               don't even know how to get one.

The words sting. Truman turns away. Seeing the pain she's
caused, she changes tack.

                         MERYL
               This'll pass. Everybody thinks like this
               now and then.
                    (making an attempt at seduction)
               Come to bed.

                         TRUMAN
               I think I'm going to stay up for a while.

35   INT. AN OFFICE BUILDING SOMEWHERE - RECEPTION. NIGHT.   35

In the reception area of an office building, TWO UNIFORMED
GUARDS drink coffee.

                         GUARD 1
               How can they have a child?

                         GUARD 2
               It's not gonna be his, you idiot.

                         GUARD 1
               Why not?

                         GUARD 2
               You think she'd go through with it?

                         GUARD 1
               Sure she would.

                         GUARD 2
                    (reassessing his own opinion)
               Guess I always thought they'd adopt.

36   EXT.   TRUMAN'S STREET.   DAWN.   36

There is something peculiar about the way the sun rises over
Seahaven Island - the light appears in an arc that's slightly
too perfect and well-defined.

37   INT.   TRUMAN'S BEDROOM.   MORNING.   37

In front of his bedroom window, TRUMAN, wearing his new
sweats, performs an exercise routine of his own invention.
He counts off the exercises to himself - cheating as he does
so. He counts five leg-lifts for every two he completes.

                    TRUMAN
          --Five...
               (two leg-lifts later)
          Ten...fifteen...two more makes twenty.

38   INT.   A BEDROOM SOMEWHERE.   MORNING.   38

A middle-aged MARRIED COUPLE in identical matching sweats
repeat the same eccentric exercises in perfect sync, as if
they were in a class led by Truman.

39   EXT.   CAR.   DAY.   39

TRUMAN climbs into the car and switches on the radio.   He drives
down the street.

                    RADIO ANNOUNCER
          Another glorious morning in Seahaven, folks.
          Don't forget to buckle up--

Truman mutters to himself as is his custom.

40   EXT.   DOWNTOWN SEAHAVEN.   DAY.   40

TRUMAN emerges from the parking lot and as usual stops at the
newspaper stand. He picks up a glossy magazine and flips
through the cosmetic ads, surreptitiously tearing a pair of
EYES from one of the pages. He returns the magazine to the
rack. As usual, the NEWSPAPER VENDOR fails to intervene.
Truman begins his daily pilgrimage to work through the rush
hour pedestrian traffic.

As he enters the street leading to his office, he glimpses a
HOMELESS MAN reflected in the window of a parked car.
Truman, spellbound by the man, suddenly wheels around to face
him. The Homeless Man, late-fifties, more well-groomed and

                                              (CONTINUED)

40   CONTINUED: 40

well-fed than the average vagrant, has a serene smile on his
face.

The Homeless Man places his hand ever so gently on Truman's
cheek. Truman makes no effort to withdraw. He is transfixed
by the man's eyes. He appears to recognize him.

                    TRUMAN
              (almost to himself, mouthing
              the word)
         Dad...

Suddenly an ELEGANT WOMAN SHOPPER walking a small WIENER DOG
and a BUSINESS EXECUTIVE carrying a briefcase, walking in
opposite directions along the sidewalk, grab the Homeless
Man. One under each arm, lifting the Homeless Man off the
ground, they start to whisk the bewildered derelict down the
street.

                    TRUMAN
              (calling out)
         Stop! Stop!!

Truman begins to give chase. However, the shopper and the
businessman are surprisingly fleet-footed.   Even more
surprising as Truman embarks on the pursuit is the behavior
of the PEDESTRIANS and COMMUTERS. They appear to part for
the fleeing trio then close ranks in front of him. Is it
accidental, or are the pedestrians working together, running
interference?

                    TRUMAN
              (shouting at the pedestrians)
         Outta the way! Outta the way!

They are escaping.

Truman finally breaks through the pack, bowling over several
of the pedestrians in the process. Just as he gets within
reach of the shopper and the businessman, a bus suddenly
screeches to a halt beside the abductors, doors already open.
The Woman Shopper and the Executive bundle the Homeless Man
onto the bus. Truman lurches after them, but he is met by
the bus doors, closing sharply in his face.

                    TRUMAN
              (to BUS DRIVER)
         Hey, stop! Stop the bus!!

Truman thumps against the doors, but the BUS DRIVER ignores
his cries and the bus roars away. The other PASSENGERS in
the bus, apparently oblivious to the incident, keep staring
straight ahead.

                                              (CONTINUED)

40   CONTINUED: (2)   40

Truman continues to give chase when a taxi appears out of
nowhere and cuts in front of him, blocking his path. When he
recovers, the bus has disappeared. The mysterious crowd of
pedestrians has also dissolved as if it never existed.

Retracing his steps, head reeling, wondering if he could have
imagined the whole incident, Truman discovers that the Woman
Shopper has left her WIENER DOG behind. The dog wanders
aimlessly on the pavement, its leash trailing behind it.

41   INT. MOTHER'S HOUSE. DAY.   41

TRUMAN paces impatiently in the living room of his Mother's
cramped, fussy, doilyed little house full of Burbank family
memorabilia - a cluster of framed photographs is dominated by
one of his FATHER trimmed with a black ribbon. A toilet
flushes and Truman's MOTHER finally emerges from the next
room.

She presents something of a contradiction. Although she
walks with the aid of a "walker", she is actually a well-
preserved sixty. She wears a glamorous nightgown and a full
head of bleached-blonde hair.

                    TRUMAN
              (kissing Mother on the cheek)
          How are you, Mother?

                    MOTHER
          Well, I made it through another night.

                    TRUMAN
          How's your hip?

                    MOTHER
          Oh, just so.

Truman supports Mother.

                    MOTHER
          You know surprises aren't good for me.
          You should really call before you come
          over, dear.

                    TRUMAN
          I've got something to tell you. You'd
          better sit down.

Truman helps her into an overstuffed armchair.

                                                      (CONTINUED)

41   CONTINUED: 41

                         MOTHER
          You look very pale, Truman. Are you
          taking your vitamin D's?

                         TRUMAN
               (exasperated)
          I spend half my life out in the sun,
          Mother, why would I need vitamin D?

                         MOTHER
          I feel certain my condition runs in the
          family.
               (putting the back of her hand
               dramatically to her forehead)
          Can't this wait, dear?

He kneels beside her.

                         TRUMAN
          No, I'm afraid it can't.

Truman takes a deep breath as he prepares to give her the news.

                         TRUMAN
          I know this is going to sound insane,
          Mother, but...I saw Dad today on
          Lancaster Circle. He's alive.

Mother smiles condescendingly.

                         MOTHER
          It doesn't sound insane, Truman. I swear
          I see him ten times a week--in a hundred
          faces. I almost hugged a perfect stranger
          in the salon last Thursday.

                         TRUMAN
          It was Dad, I swear, dressed like a
          homeless man. And you know what else was
          really strange? A businessman and a
          woman with a little dog appeared from
          nowhere and forced him onto a bus.

                         MOTHER
          About time they started cleaning up the
          trash Downtown. We don't want to end up
          like the rest of the country.

                         TRUMAN
               (excited)
          They never found Dad's body - maybe
          somehow--

(CONTINUED)

41   CONTINUED: (2)   41

                          MOTHER
                 --Darling--

                          TRUMAN
                 (already doubting himself)
                 I'm telling you, if it wasn't him, it was
                 his twin. Did Dad have a brother?

                          MOTHER
                 You know he was an only child, like you.
                          (placing a comforting arm
                          around him)
                 I know how bad you feel about what
                 happened--sailing into that storm. But I
                 don't blame you, Truman. I never have.

Mother kisses Truman on the cheek.

                          MOTHER
                          (referring to her platinum
                          blonde hair)
                 I was thinking about going lighter. What
                 do you think?

Truman regards his Mother. Her hair is already impossibly blonde.

42   INT. TRUMAN'S BASEMENT. DUSK.   42

The basement is cluttered with junk - ships in bottles, a
train track without trains, an oxygen mask, a stringless
guitar, many abandoned projects. The basement is dimly lit
by a single, naked bulb. TRUMAN looks over his shoulder
before opening a large walk-in cupboard. On the cupboard
door is a wall map of the Pacific Ocean - the Fiji Islands
are carefully circled. Amongst the many tools and household
implements inside the cupboard is a trunk under a dusty
canvas sheet. He pulls the trunk into the room, unfastens
the lock and opens the lid.

Inside, mementoes from his youth. A *"HOW TO SAIL"* book, a
stack of *"GREAT EXPLORERS"* magazines, and beneath it all, a
garment in a drycleaning bag. Truman carefully lifts up the
plastic to reveal a young woman's cardigan sweater. He puts
the cardigan to his nose and takes in its scent.

Footsteps. Truman hastily drops the cardigan in the trunk
and shuts the lid. MERYL's legs appear on the stairs.

                          MERYL
                 What're you doing down here?

                                                        (CONTINUED)

42   CONTINUED: 42

>   TRUMAN
>   (turning attention to an upturned
>   mower on the basement floor)
>   Fixing the mower.
>   (matter-of-fact)
>   I saw my father today.
>
>   MERYL
>   I know.
>
>   TRUMAN
>   (suspicious)
>   How do you know?
>
>   MERYL
>   Your mother called. You shouldn't upset
>   her like that.

Meryl's response takes the wind out of Truman's sails.

>   TRUMAN
>   What did you want?
>
>   MERYL
>   I made macaroni.
>
>   TRUMAN
>   I'm not hungry.

Meryl nods, not at all convinced.

>   MERYL
>   We really ought to toss that mower out.
>   Get one of those new Elk Rotaries.

Truman does not reply. After an uncomfortable pause, she
turns back up the stairs.

Truman waits a moment before re-opening the trunk. He
removes the cardigan and holds it up, reminiscing.

43   INT. A KITCHEN SOMEWHERE. NIGHT.   43

A MOTHER, DAUGHTER about 12, and a BABY in a highchair stare
into camera.

>   DAUGHTER
>   What's he doing?
>
>   MOTHER
>   They removed all physical trace of her
>   but they couldn't erase the memory.

43   CONTINUED: 43

                              DAUGHTER
                    The memory of who?

                              MOTHER
                         (finger to lips)
                    Shhh!

44   *PLAYBACK MONTAGE - EXT. COLLEGE CAMPUS - STEPS. DAY.*   44

       Once again the images appear to be playing on a television screen.

       On the steps of a typical college campus, TRUMAN, 21, in a
       college band uniform, participates in a football pep rally.
       MARLON, 21, a member of the football team, and MERYL, 21, a
       cheerleader, are nearby. Truman observes an ethereal-looking
       young woman walk by - LAUREN.

44A   *PLAYBACK - INT. DANCEHALL. NIGHT.*   44A

       At a college dance, TRUMAN dances with MERYL. LAUREN dances
       by with a PARTNER of her own. However, Truman only has eyes
       for Lauren. Suddenly, she is escorted from the dance floor.

44B   *PLAYBACK - EXT. COLLEGE CAMPUS - STREET. DAY.*   44B

       TRUMAN almost trips off the curb as he waves to LAUREN,
       riding towards him on a bicycle. However, she rides right by
       with her nose in the air, not even acknowledging his presence
       - Truman puzzled by her change of heart.

       The montage ends at a scene in a college library.

45   *PLAYBACK - INT. COLLEGE LIBRARY. NIGHT.*   45

       In the school library, TRUMAN, 21, sits with MARLON, 21, and
       wife-to-be, MERYL, 21, doing a final cram for a test. The
       STUDENTS begin to pack up their books. Meryl gives Truman a
       peck on the cheek.

                              MERYL
                    Come on, Truman. Haven't you studied
                    enough?

                              TRUMAN
                    I still want to look over a couple of
                    things.

                                                      (CONTINUED)

45   CONTINUED: 45

                        MARLON
                    (punching Truman in a chummy
                    way on the arm, referring to
                    Truman's books)
            Take the "C" average. That's what I do.

Truman looks up from his books. The library is almost
deserted. He spies a GIRL's hand around the table divider.

Truman musters the nerve to poke his head over the divider. He
finds LAUREN on the other side, buried in a book.

                        TRUMAN
                Konichi-wa.

Lauren looks blank.

                        TRUMAN
                    (referring to the Japanese
                    text in front of her)
                You take Japanese.

                        LAUREN
                    (quickly closing the book)
                Oh, yes.

                        TRUMAN
                    (glancing to the name carefully
                    written on the front of the book)
                Lauren, right?

                        LAUREN
                    (as if unaware of her own name)
                That's right. Lauren.

                        TRUMAN
                    (extending his hand)
                I'm Truman, Truman Burbank--

                        LAUREN
                --I'm not allowed to talk to you.

Truman is not surprised.

                        TRUMAN
                    (resigned)
                It's okay. I probably wouldn't talk to
                me either.

                        LAUREN
                    (softening)
                I'm sorry. It's not up to me.

                                                    (CONTINUED)

45   CONTINUED: (2)   45

                        TRUMAN
                   (crestfallen)
              You have a boyfriend? Of course you do.

Lauren looks about her, unsure.

                        LAUREN
              No...I, er.

                        TRUMAN
                   (hopeful once again)
              No? Really? Good, I mean, I thought
              possibly a pizza. How about Friday?

                        LAUREN
              No.

                        TRUMAN
              Saturday?

Lauren looks around the almost-deserted library.

                        TRUMAN
              Actually, I'm free Sunday.

                        LAUREN
              Now.

                        TRUMAN
              Right now? We've got finals tomorrow.

                        LAUREN
              If we don't go now, it won't happen.

Truman hesitates.

                        LAUREN
                   (impatient, looking anxiously
                    around)
              Well, what do you want to do?

                        TRUMAN
                   (closing his books, still a
                    little uncertain)
              I think I've studied enough.

46   *PLAYBACK* - EXT. VARIOUS LOCATIONS NEAR SEAHAVEN COLLEGE. NIGHT. 46

LAUREN, taking TRUMAN by the hand, runs down various streets
and paths through the campus. She occasionally pauses and
looks about her, often changing direction or looking up at
streetlights and the towers of houses along their route, as
if trying to elude an unseen pursuer.

                                              (CONTINUED)

46   CONTINUED: 46

The excited and apprehensive Truman runs with her although he
is unsure exactly who, or what, they are running from.

The further they get from the campus, the higher, wider and
less effective the coverage of the scene - some camera angles
are even partially obscured.

47   *PLAYBACK - EXT. HIGHWAY - WESTERN END OF TOWN. NIGHT.*   47

TRUMAN and LAUREN eventually cross an empty highway on the edge
of town.

They run over the dunes onto a strangely deserted beach and
down to the water's edge under a hyper-real full moon.
Lauren throws off her cardigan and hitches up her skirt,
wading out into the inviting water without another thought.
Truman stares down, transfixed by the shimmering water.

                    LAUREN
                (splashing)
        It's beautiful! What are you waiting for?

                    TRUMAN
                (nervous)
        I...I can't.

Lauren suddenly stops splashing.

                    LAUREN
        That's right. Oh, God, I'm sorry.

She wades out of the water.

                    TRUMAN
                (confused)
        Why, Lauren? You've got nothing to be
        sorry about?

Lauren, dripping wet, stands beside Truman at the shoreline. She
meets his gaze.

                    LAUREN
        My name's not Lauren. It's Sylvia.

Truman looks into her eyes and believes her. Truman wipes
the water from her face, then leans forward and gently kisses
her lips. She kisses him back.

48   INT. A BAR SOMEWHERE. NIGHT.   48

In a quiet bar room, a WAITRESS explains her viewpoint to the
BARMAN. A PATRON on a barstool eavesdrops.

                    WAITRESS
          Don't you get it? She was willing to lose
          him, lose everything, if it meant he could
          find himself.
                    (registering the barman's blank look)
          Never mind. You wouldn't understand.

49   *PLAYBACK* - EXT. BEACH. NIGHT.   49

As we return to Truman's reminiscence, TRUMAN and SYLVIA (as
she is now called throughout the remainder of the movie) sit
on the sand at the water's edge. With great delicacy, Truman
traces the outline of her nose with his finger, at the same
time inhaling her scent. Sylvia looks nervously around her.
Truman goes to say something but Sylvia hushes him.

                    SYLVIA
          They're coming. Any minute.

                    TRUMAN
                    (looking around the deserted beach)
          Who?

                    SYLVIA
          They're going to stop me talking to you.

                    TRUMAN
                    (confused)
          There's no one here.

                    SYLVIA
                    (looking over her shoulder
                    nervously)
          Just listen. You remember when you were a
          little boy, you stood up in class and
          said you wanted to be an explorer like
          Magellan--

                    TRUMAN
                    (incredulous)
          --How do you know about that?

                    SYLVIA
          --And your teacher said, "You're too late,
          Truman. There's nothing left to explore."

                                                        (CONTINUED)

> TRUMAN
> Were you there--how do you know?

> SYLVIA
> --It doesn't matter. Everybody knows
> about it. They know everything you do.
> The point is, you got scared.

> TRUMAN
> I don't understand.

> SYLVIA
> (looking over her shoulder,
> increasingly nervous)
> You must listen. Everybody's pretending,
> Truman.

She points to the sky and scoops up the sea water at their feet.

> SYLVIA
> You think this is real? It's all for
> you. A show.
> (frustrated, raving)
> The eyes are everywhere. They're
> watching you - *right now*.

Suddenly a car's headlights come bouncing over the dunes.
The car roars across the beach towards the couple.

> SYLVIA
> (scared)
> I told you, Truman!

The car skids to a stop and a large MAN, 40ish, with a shock of
red hair, jumps from the car. The man yanks the frightened
Sylvia to her feet, causing her cardigan to fall to the ground.

> MAN
> (to Sylvia, oddly sympathetic)
> Lauren, sweetheart, not again. Get in
> the car!

Truman jumps up.

> TRUMAN
> Hey, who the hell are you?!

> MAN
> I'm her father!

> TRUMAN
> We weren't doing anything.

49   CONTINUED: (2)   49

                         SYLVIA
                 He's not my father! He's just saying
                 that! Does he look anything like me?!

                         MAN
                 Come on, Sweetheart.

The Man gently, but firmly, pushes Sylvia towards his car. Sylvia
resists. Truman crosses to them.

                         TRUMAN
                 I'll take care of her!

The Man takes Truman aside and whispers in his ear.

                         MAN
                     (whispered, out of Sylvia's earshot)
                 Schizophrenia. She has episodes.

Doubts start crowding into Truman's head.

                         SYLVIA
                     (calling out from the car)
                 Don't listen to him, Truman. I'm telling you
                 the truth!

                         MAN
                     (getting into the car)
                 Don't bother! We're moving to...*Fiji - the
                 Fiji Islands!* This place has done
                 something to her head.

50   INT. A DIMLY-LIT ROOM SOMEWHERE. NIGHT - *PRESENT*.   50

CHRISTOF stares intently into camera. Beside him is his
assistant, CHLOE, an androgenous-looking young woman. She
too stares into camera.

                         CHRISTOF
                 At least he didn't say "New York City".

51   *PLAYBACK* - EXT. BEACH. NIGHT.   51

TRUMAN stares after the car as it roars away. He turns back
toward the ocean where his attention is caught by an object
lying on the sand - Sylvia's cardigan.

52   INT.   TRUMAN'S BASEMENT.   NIGHT - *PRESENT*.   52

TRUMAN carefully places the cardigan back into the trunk.

53   INT.   A KITCHEN SOMEWHERE.   NIGHT.   53

MOTHER, DAUGHTER and BABY stare into camera.

> DAUGHTER
> But why didn't he just follow her
> to Fiji?

> MOTHER
> Because his mother got sick - very,
> sick. He couldn't leave her. He's a
> kind boy, maybe too kind.

> DAUGHTER
> I can't believe he married Meryl on
> the rebound.

54   INT.   BASEMENT.   NIGHT.   54

TRUMAN turns his attention to the framed photograph of Meryl
that he carries everywhere. Hidden behind her photo is a
composite picture of Sylvia which Truman has constructed by
pasting together individual facial features - nose, mouth, ears,
chin, hair - gathered, presumably, from women's magazines. He
attempts to put the jigsaw puzzle together - although he has
particular difficulty finding a pair of eyes that match.

From his pocket he takes a recent collection of eyes which,
like a detective working on an identikit picture, he tries to
match. They are still not quite right.

55   INT.   AN APARTMENT SOMEWHERE.   NIGHT.   55

The eyes of a YOUNG WOMAN - blue-green eyes. She turns
slightly, looking directly into camera. We pull back to
reveal her face - SYLVIA.

56   EXT.   TRUMAN'S STREET.   EARLY MORNING.   56

Dawn breaks over Truman's street. On cue, the sound of birds.

57   EXT.   STREET OUTSIDE TRUMAN'S HOUSE.   MORNING.   57

TRUMAN leaves the house, lost in thought. SPENCER is taking
out the trash.

                    SPENCER
               How's it going, Truman?

Truman hardly acknowledges Spencer. PLUTO the dog fails to
receive his usual pat. The wave from the WASHINGTON's across
the street is also not returned.

58   INT/EXT.   CAR/STREET OUTSIDE TRUMAN'S HOUSE.   DAY.   58

TRUMAN motors down the street, switching on the car radio
as usual.

                    RADIO ANNOUNCER
               --Don't forget to buckle up out there in
               radioland. It's another glorious...
               ..morrrninggg...innn... Seaaaa...
               haaaa...vennnn...f...o...l...k...s...

The Announcer's voice slows down - now revealing itself to be
a tape that has worn out. Truman, perplexed, looks at the
radio and pushes buttons in an attempt to find another
station. He finds one.

                    FEMALE VOICE
                    (from radio)
               ...west on Stewart...he's making a right
               on Holden...

Truman glances up at the street signs along his route and
finds that they correspond exactly with the streets quoted
on the radio. Distracted, he almost bowls over an OLD LADY
on a crosswalk.

                    MALE VOICE
                    (from radio)
               ...God, he almost hit Marilyn!...He's on
               the move again, passing the library...

Truman readjusts the radio as it starts to fade out.
Suddenly, there is a piercing blast of feedback. He looks up
and, as far as the eye can see, every PEDESTRIAN, MOTORIST
and SHOPKEEPER along the street suddenly winces in pain and
holds their right ear at exactly the same moment.

(CONTINUED)

58 CONTINUED: 58

                              MALE VOICE
                    (from radio, in distress himself)
                 ...Something's wrong. Change frequencies...

Truman tries to pick up the channel once again but without
success.

59 EXT. PARKING LOT. MORNING.   59

TRUMAN sits in his car, drinking his coffee, taking in the
recent incident. From inside the adjacent school, he hears
the familiar, excited squeals and chatter of SCHOOL CHILDREN.
Truman suddenly throws aside his coffee and sprints across
the parking lot and into the school.

60 INT. SEAHAVEN ELEMENTARY SCHOOL. MORNING.   60

TRUMAN slams through the front doors into the reception area.
It is deserted, no one stationed at the administration desk,
the corridors empty. He runs down a vacant corridor, finally
standing outside a classroom. The childrens' voices can
still be heard from inside. Truman bursts through the door.

The room is empty save for a large reel-to-reel tape recorder
on the teacher's desk playing a continuous tape of childrens'
voices. The recorder is attached to speakers on tall stands
facing the ventilation ducts. Truman stares at the machine
in disbelief.

61 EXT. STREET - DOWNTOWN. DAY.   61

TRUMAN, still lost in thought, exits the school. He stops at
the newsstand and picks up a magazine to resume his ritual
search but his heart is not in it. He replaces the magazine
without taking a cutting - much to the surprise of the NEWS
VENDOR.

Truman starts his trek to work, pausing to stare at his
reflection in the mirrored building, hoping that the Homeless
Man will appear once again at his side. No one joins him.

62 EXT. DOWNTOWN STREET. DAY.   62

Entering his own building with fellow OFFICE WORKERS, TRUMAN
remains in the revolving door and re-emerges on the street.

63   EXT. CITY STREETS. DAY.   63

TRUMAN wanders aimlessly through a city park, observing. We
sense, truly observing for the first time.

A YOUNG WOMAN walks a pair of AFGHAN HOUNDS. An OLD MAN
answers the incessant questions of his GRANDCHILD. Nothing
appears amiss. Truman takes a seat at a small, outdoor cafe.
He fidgets with his father's ring on his finger that contains
one large stone, still looking for a false move.

A DELIVERY MAN unloads boxes from the back of his truck and
carries them into a store. Further down the street
CONSTRUCTION WORKERS take their time tending to an electrical
repair in an exposed manhole. A POSTAL WORKER does his
rounds. An OLD WOMAN struggles with two heavy shopping bags.
Everybody appears natural, places to go.

64   INT. A DIMLY-LIT ROOM SOMEWHERE. DAY.   64

CHRISTOF and CHLOE stare into camera. Christof leans forward
and speaks.

                    CHRISTOF
          ...Everybody stay focussed. Remember who
          you are.

65   EXT. CAFE. DAY   65

TRUMAN turns his attention to a group of CUBAN-LOOKING MEN at
the only other occupied table at the cafe. We see extreme
close-ups as Truman scans the men's faces for any sign of
phoniness. They are talking loudly, making suggestive
comments to the WAITRESS. Their behavior passes the test -
all seems genuine.

Then, Truman notices TWO JOGGERS out for a morning run,
making their way down the street towards him. Truman happens
to glance at the sneakers of one of the joggers. He suddenly
springs to his feet. Truman blocks the joggers.

                    TRUMAN
          It's you...isn't it?

The Joggers attempt to sidestep Truman.

                    JOGGER 1
          Excuse me.

                                                        (CONTINUED)

65   CONTINUED: 65

                              TRUMAN
                    Remember? Two days ago I gave you my
                    meatball sandwich in the park. You were
                    in a wheelchair. Same sneakers.

The jogger looks down at his distinctive sneakers bearing the
initials, "T.S.", and visibly blanches.

                              JOGGER 2
                         (coming to his companion's aid)
                    Get the hell out of here.

The second jogger roughly shoves Truman aside. Truman calls
out after the two men.

                              TRUMAN
                         (ironically referring to the
                         Jogger's new-found mobility)
                    It's a miracle!

Truman picks himself up, dusting dirt from his suit. He
retrieves his briefcase and continues down the street with
renewed purpose.

66   EXT. DOWNTOWN STREET. DAY.   66

Wandering down the bustling street, TRUMAN suddenly bolts
into a building at random.

67   INT. OFFICE BUILDING. DAY.   67

An imposing office building clad in the kind of reflective
glass that shields its occupants from the world - a building
Truman passes every day. A steady stream of EMPLOYEES and
VISITORS enter and exit the building's high-ceilinged lobby
past an intimidating security desk manned by TWO UNIFORMED
GUARDS. Beyond security are banks of elevators, ferrying
executives, clerical staff and delivery personnel to and from
their floors of business.

Truman abruptly enters reception and strides confidently
past the security desk trying to look as if he belongs.

                         SECURITY GUARD 1
                         (to Truman)
                    Can I help?

                              TRUMAN
                         (sneaking a glance at the
                         building directory)
                    I have an appointment at, er...Gable
                    Enterprises.

                                                        (CONTINUED)

> SECURITY GUARD 1
> They went bust.

The second Security Guard is rising from his seat to block Truman's path to the elevators but Truman reads his mind and makes a dash for it - into one of the elevators.

A YOUNG WOMAN in the elevator looks in horror at Truman - the cause of her concern all too apparent. Looking beyond the Woman, Truman discovers that there is no back to the elevator car. The PEOPLE Truman has just witnessed entering other elevators are milling around a refreshment table, primping or sitting on folding chairs. Gradually, they all turn to gape at Truman, who in turn stares back, appalled. Truman's view is abruptly blocked as a rear panel is hastily attached to the elevator. A Security Guard pulls Truman from the car.

> TRUMAN
> What's going on?

> SECURITY GUARD 1
> (glancing to the lights above
> the elevator, trying to appear
> innocent)
> Nothing.

Truman observes the upward progress of the elevator via the light display above the doorway. Before he has time to make sense of it, the guards drag him away.

> SECURITY GUARD 2
> You've got to leave.

The Guards frog-march Truman out of the facade towards an Emergency Exit.

> TRUMAN
> Just tell me what's going on?

> SECURITY GUARD 2
> We're re-modelling.

> TRUMAN
> No you're not!! What were those people
> doing in there?

> SECURITY GUARD 1
> (shrugs)
> It's none of my business.
> (ushering Truman off the
> property)
> None of *yours*, either.

(CONTINUED)

67   CONTINUED: (2)   67

                              TRUMAN
                        (not going quietly)
                   You don't tell me what's really going on,
                   I'll report you.

TRUMAN continues to struggle as the GUARDS usher him to the
street.

                         SECURITY GUARD 2
                   For what? You're trespassing!

68   EXT. DOWNTOWN STREET. DAY.   68

TRUMAN continues to struggle as the GUARDS unceremoniously
dump him on the pavement. He picks himself up, head reeling,
and starts to run along the street. He suddenly enters
another building at random. An office block with a bank on
the ground floor.

Truman rushes to the elevators. The lights above the doors
show all the elevators on upper floors. Frantic pressing of
the elevator button gets no response. A RECEPTIONIST rises
from her desk. Truman heads for the stairs but is
intercepted by a BANK OFFICIAL barring his way.

                              TRUMAN
                   I want to...

The Bank Official, the Receptionist, and a BANK TELLER back
Truman towards the door.

                         BANK OFFICIAL
                   ...Open an account?

                              TRUMAN
                   Yes. Er, why not?

                         RECEPTIONIST
                   Savings or checking?

                         BANK OFFICIAL
                   Let's go up to my office.

Truman hurriedly exits the bank.

68A   EXT. STREET. DAY.   68A

Back on the street, TRUMAN feels the eyes of the PEDESTRIANS.
Is he simply drawing attention to himself by his behavior?
Truman wheels around, trying to make eye contact with passersby.
They shy away. He continues to run down the street.

                                               (CONTINUED)

68A   CONTINUED: 68A

Finally, Truman finds himself standing in front of the
window of an electronics store staring at his own face on a
TV set. It is taking a feed from a camcorder aimed out the
store window.

69   INT. A BATHROOM SOMEWHERE. DAY.   69

A MAN stares into camera from a bath of stale water - a layer
of soap scum on the top.

                         MAN
              Don't look at me, pal.

70   EXT. STREET - ELECTRONICS STORE. DAY.   70

TRUMAN shudders at his video reflection. Further down the
street, he notices Marlon's van parked outside a supermarket.

71   INT. SUPERMARKET. DAY.   71

The door of a vending machine is open. MARLON, half inside
the machine, loads a stack of Baby Ruth candy bars into one
of the dispensing slots. The paranoid TRUMAN appears at his
shoulder.

                         TRUMAN
              Marlon--

                         MARLON
                    (startled)
              --Truman, what are you doing here?

Truman looks nervously around him. Even the STORE OWNER's
friendly nod from behind the counter is cause for suspicion
in Truman's mind.

                         TRUMAN
                    (whisper)
              I've got to talk to you.

                         MARLON
              Sorry, I'm way behind.

                         TRUMAN
              I'm onto something, Marlon - something big.

                         MARLON
              Are you okay? You look like shit.

                                                          (CONTINUED)

> TRUMAN
> I think I'm mixed up in something.

> MARLON
> *Mixed up?* Mixed up in what?

> TRUMAN
> There's no point in trying to explain it,
> but a lot of strange things have been
> happening - elevators that don't go
> anywhere, people talking about me on the
> radio, you know what I mean?

> MARLON
> (bemused)
> No. Truman, if this is another one of
> your fantasies...

> TRUMAN
> I think it's got something to do with
> my dad.

> MARLON
> Your Dad?!

> TRUMAN
> (looking around nervously)
> I think he's alive. I'll tell you about
> it later. I'm definitely being followed.

> MARLON
> (looking around, instantly
> protective)
> Who?

> TRUMAN
> It's hard to tell. They look just like
> regular people.

> MARLON
> (referring to an OLD COUPLE
> entering the deli)
> How about them?

> TRUMAN
> (seriously considering the
> possibility)
> Could be. Beard looks phony.
> (leaning closer to Marlon)
> It's when I'm unpredictable. They can't
> stand that. That's why we've got to get
> out of here. Can you come with me?

(CONTINUED)

71   CONTINUED: (2)   71

                              MARLON
                    (closing up the vending machine)
               I told you I can't.

                              TRUMAN
               I've got to show you something.

          Truman fixes Marlon with a look of deadly seriousness.

                              MARLON
                    (weakening)
               Christ, Truman. You're gonna get both
               our asses fired.

72   EXT. SEAHAVEN ELEMENTARY SCHOOL. DAY.   72

          TRUMAN hurries MARLON up the school steps. The sound of
          children's voices continues to drift out from inside the
          building. Truman and Marlon storm into the school reception
          area - still empty.

73   INT. SCHOOL CORRIDOR. DAY.   73

          TRUMAN and MARLON stand outside the classroom, the source of
          the children's voices. Truman throws his friend an "I-told-
          you-so" look and swings open the door with a flourish.

74   INT. CLASSROOM. DAY.   74

          The once-empty classroom is now full of SCHOOL CHILDREN in an
          art class. A hush falls over the students and all eyes turn
          to TRUMAN and MARLON.

                              TEACHER
                    (gesturing to two unoccupied
                    easels)
               Would you care to join us?

75   EXT. CLIFFTOP. DUSK.   75

          Hand-over-hand, TRUMAN climbs the cliff he once scaled as a
          seven-year-old. Finally, he sits on the clifftop, staring
          out at the view his father had been so desperate for him not
          to see twenty-six years earlier. However, the deserted bay
          beyond is identical to its neighbor. MARLON, laboring,
          crests the rise and joins his friend on the clifftop.

                                                          (CONTINUED)

> MARLON
> What're we doing here, Truman?

> TRUMAN
> This is where it started.

> MARLON
> What exactly?

> TRUMAN
> Things. Things that don't fit.
>   (another thought occurs)
> Maybe I'm being set up for something.
> You ever feel like that, Marlon? Like
> your whole life has been building to
> something?

> MARLON
>   (blank)
> No.

> TRUMAN
>   (ignoring the remark)
> When you were hauling chickens for Kaiser
> Poultry, what was the furthest you ever
> went off the island?

> MARLON
> I went all over but I never found a place
> like this.
>   (nodding to the setting sun)
> Look at that sunset, Truman. It's perfect.

> TRUMAN
>   (in a daze)
> Yeah...

> MARLON
>   (glancing heavenwards)
> That's the "Big Guy". Quite a paintbrush
> he's got.

> TRUMAN
> Just between you and me, Marlon, I'm
> going away for a while.

> MARLON
> Really?

76   INT. LIVING ROOM - TRUMAN'S HOUSE. NIGHT.   76

TRUMAN sits cramped on his sofa. Pulling wider, we discover
the cause of his discomfort. He is sandwiched between MERYL
on one side and MOTHER on the other. Mother, the family
historian, a stack of photograph albums at her feet, turns
the pages of the album on Truman's lap.

                    TRUMAN
          We ought to be getting you back, Mother.

                    MOTHER
          Hold on a minute, Dear.
                    (pointing out a photo in the album)
          Here's us at Mount Rushmore. You
          remember, Truman--when Dad was still with
          us--that was quite a drive. You slept
          all the way there.

                    TRUMAN
                    (taking an interest in the
                    monument)
          It looks so small.

                    MOTHER
                    (quickly turning the page)
          Things always do--when you look back.

Mother skips several pages in the album, finally stopping at
a spread of wedding photos.

                    MERYL
          Look, Truman, there's my cousin Errol
          putting the bouquet down his pants - it
          was the happiest day of our lives.

                    MOTHER
                    (referring to Meryl)
          Didn't she look beautiful, Truman? She
          still does.

Mother turns to a blank page in the album.

                    MOTHER
          And there's plenty of room for baby
          photos. I'd like to hold a grandchild
          in my arms--
                    (dabbing her eye with a handkerchief)
          --before I go.

Meryl rises from the sofa and helps Mother to her walker.

                                                    (CONTINUED)

76   CONTINUED: 76

                         MERYL
          I'll take you home, Angela.
               (referring to the albums)
          Why don't you leave those with us for
          a while?

                         TRUMAN
               (kissing his emotional mother)
          Good night, Mother.

                         MERYL
               (a wink to Truman)
          See you in a minute, sweetheart.

Meryl departs with Mother. Left alone in the living room,
Truman slumps back down onto the sofa and switches on the
television set - an old-fashioned model with rabbit-ears.
He idly studies the photograph album as an over-earnest
television HOST announces the upcoming program.

                         TV HOST
          --Tonight's golden-oldie is the
          enduring, much-loved classic, "Show Me
          The Way To Go Home". A hymn of praise
          to small-town life where we learn that
          you don't have to leave home to
          discover what the world is all about
          and that no one is poor who has
          friends...

However, when we turn our attention away from the
television, we find that Truman is peering intently at a
wedding photograph of Meryl and himself taking their vows in
a civil ceremony in a beachside gazebo. Under the scrutiny
of a magnifying glass, he discovers that Meryl has her
fingers crossed.

77   INT. A LIVING ROOM SOMEWHERE. NIGHT.   77

The TWO OLD LADIES sit on their sofa, a rug across their
knees, sipping a night cap of hot chocolate. They stare into
camera.

                         OLD LADY 1
          Remember at the wedding - that dog?

                         OLD LADY 2
          Started howling when they took their vows.

                                                    (CONTINUED)

77   CONTINUED: 77

> OLD LADY 1
> And the plastic horseshoe fell off when
> they cut the cake.

> OLD LADY 2
> (shaking her head ruefully)
> They never had a chance.

78   INT. KITCHEN. MORNING.   78

TRUMAN, dressed casually in weekend attire, is at the stove
preparing an omelette. MERYL hurries into the kitchen in her
nurse's uniform. She gulps down a cup of coffee and reaches
for her nurse's cap.

However, she still has time to adjust the position of a pack of
"FibreCon Cereal" - squaring it a little more to camera.

> TRUMAN
> I have to talk with you.
> (looking about, suspicious)
> But not here. Let's go for a walk.

> MERYL
> (kissing him on the cheek)
> I'm sorry, I'm late.

> TRUMAN
> What's the hurry?

> MERYL
> Surgery. The elevator disaster downtown
> on the news last night. Cable snapped, a
> car dropped ten floors. Non-union
> contractors. Monsters. We're starting
> with an amputation.

Truman's eyes widen. Meryl adjusts her hat in the mirror.

> MERYL
> That building's near yours. Imagine if
> you'd been in there for some reason. It
> doesn't bear thinking about.

Truman, lost in thought, picks up the scalding frying pan with
his bare hand. Letting out a howl of pain, he drops the pan.

> TRUMAN
> Arrah!

(CONTINUED)

78   CONTINUED: 78

                         MERYL
               Oh, my God!

                         TRUMAN
               What do I do?

                         MERYL
               I don't know--

                         TRUMAN
               --you're a nurse, aren't you?

                         MERYL
               Put some butter on it--or ice?

She looks up at the kitchen clock.

                         MERYL
                    (hurrying out the door)
               Oh, look at the time.

Truman stares after her, the pain of his hand forgotten for the
moment. He watches Meryl ride her bicycle down the driveway.
Truman exits the house.

79   EXT. SEAHAVEN STREETS/HOSPITAL/PARKING LOT. DAY.   79

Riding a bicycle of his own, TRUMAN follows MERYL to work,
staying a safe distance back. He watches her enter the
hospital.

80   INT. HOSPITAL. DAY.   80

TRUMAN makes his way along various corridors. All seems as
it should - DOCTORS confer with NURSING STAFF and PATIENTS,
gurneys are wheeled about with their PASSENGERS looking
suitably traumatized. Truman approaches a NURSING SISTER.

                         TRUMAN
               I'm looking for my wife--Nurse Burbank.
               It's important.

                         NURSE
                    (checking her clipboard)
               I'm afraid that's impossible--she's in pre-op.

                         TRUMAN
               Sure. Okay. Fine. Can you pass on a
               message?

                                                        (CONTINUED)

80   CONTINUED: 80

                         NURSE
               I'll try.

                         TRUMAN
               Tell her, tell her...I had to go to Fiji.
               I'll call her when I get there.

                         NURSE
               When you get to Fiji?

                         TRUMAN
               You got it.

                         NURSE
               Fine. I'll tell her.

          The nurse walks off, disappearing through a set of doors.
          Truman hesitates before following her.

81   INT. VARIOUS HOSPITAL CORRIDORS. DAY.   81

          The NURSE walks briskly - fewer people about, TRUMAN
          discreetly following behind. The nurse breaks into a jog.
          Truman hurries to keep up with her - dodging around gurneys,
          JANITORS mopping floors.

82   INT. OUTSIDE OPERATING THEATRE. DAY.   82

          The NURSE, hastily scrubbed and gowned, enters the theatre. TRUMAN
          hesitates but dares not enter. He grabs a mask of his own.

          Looking through the glass window in the operating theatre
          door, he sees the YOUNG WOMAN (seen in the hastily fixed
          elevator car the day before) lying on the operating table, a
          blood-soaked bandage covering her left leg. MERYL, wearing a
          surgical gown and mask, assists the SURGEON. The SISTER
          hovers nervously in the background.

                         SURGEON
               Scalpel.

          Meryl very slowly selects a scalpel from a tray of instruments
          and awkwardly hands it to the surgeon.

                         SURGEON
               I'm now making my primary incision just
               above the left knee.

          The patient's eyes blink open in horror. The ANESTHETIST
          steps in Truman's view before he can get a good look.
          Suddenly, a SECURITY GUARD appears beside Truman and takes
          him by the arm.

                                                      (CONTINUED)

82   CONTINUED: 82

                        SECURITY GUARD
                    (referring to the operation)
            This isn't gonna be pretty. Unless
            you're family of the patient, I'll have
            to ask you to leave.

                        TRUMAN
            No problem. I don't want to cause any
            trouble.

83   INT. TRAVEL AGENCY. DAY.   83

TRUMAN takes a seat at the only desk in an empty travel
agency. The travel brochures and posters that adorn the
walls all feature destinations that bear a striking
similarity to picturesque Seahaven. Another poster spells
out the dangers of travel - *"TRAVELLERS BEWARE - Terrorists,
Disease, Wild Animals, Street Gangs"*. A female TRAVEL AGENT
enters from a rear door.

                        AGENT
            I'm sorry to keep you. How can I help?

                        TRUMAN
            I want to book a flight to Fiji.

                        AGENT
            Where exactly?

                        TRUMAN
                    (believing she is being
                    deliberately obtuse)
            Fiji.

                        AGENT
                    (a trace of condescension)
            Where in Fiji? What island?

                        TRUMAN
            I'm, sorry, er,...the biggest one.

                        AGENT
                    (entering the destination in
                    her computer)
            Viti Levu. For how many?

                        TRUMAN
                    (finding the question suspicious)
            One.

                                                    (CONTINUED)

83   CONTINUED: 83

> AGENT
> When do you want to leave, remembering, of
> course, you do lose a day on the way there?

> TRUMAN
> Today.

> AGENT
> (reading off her computer screen)
> I'm sorry. I don't have anything for at
> least a month.

> TRUMAN
> (suspicious)
> *A month.*

> AGENT
> (patiently explaining)
> It's the busy season.

> TRUMAN
> (paranoia showing)
> You are a travel agent, aren't you?
> (reading her nametag)
> "Doris"? Your job is to help people
> travel.

> AGENT
> (showing amazing restraint)
> I do have a fabulous rate on a cruise
> ship departing for Fiji tomorrow. But
> you wouldn't want to do that.

> TRUMAN
> Why wouldn't I?

> AGENT
> I thought you were in a hurry.

> TRUMAN
> (calming down)
> That's right.

> AGENT
> You want to book the flight?

> TRUMAN
> It doesn't matter. I'll make other
> arrangements.

84   EXT. CITY STREET. DAY.   84

Emerging onto the street, TRUMAN looks across to the building
which he entered the previous day. It is now cordoned off
with police tape after the elevator disaster. Flowers have
been laid at the doorway.

85   EXT. GREYHOUND BUS STATION. DAY.   85

A Greyhound Bus, bound for "CHICAGO" according to its
destination sign, sits idling at the stop. Just as a burly
SUPERVISOR is about to wave the bus on its way, TRUMAN dashes
into the station.

                    BUS DRIVER
              Last call for Chicago.

Truman jumps onto the bus behind the last boarding passenger
- a YOUNG SOLDIER.

                    TRUMAN
               (to the Bus Driver, as he
               boards the bus)
              Windy City, here we come.

86   INT. GREYHOUND BUS. DAY.   86

TRUMAN takes a seat by a window. An awkward silence descends
over the bus. The other passengers - a MOTHER with a
restless CHILD, several TOURISTS, an OLD COUPLE and the YOUNG
SOLDIER - all stare stiffly straight ahead, averting their
eyes from Truman.

No one is more uncomfortable than the BUS DRIVER. Beads of
perspiration on his head, he fumbles for the gear shift,
apparently unsure how to operate it. The gears grind.

The OTHER PASSENGERS try not to notice. The CHILD, tugging
her MOTHER's sleeve, points to Truman. Her mother makes her
face the front of the bus. Finally the SUPERVISOR enters the
bus.

                    SUPERVISOR
              Everybody off. We've got a problem.

The relieved passengers hurriedly exit until Truman is the
only one remaining on the bus. The Bus Driver looks almost
sorry for Truman who sits resolutely in his seat - the hint
of a tear of frustration in his eyes.

                                              (CONTINUED)

86   CONTINUED: 86

                         BUS DRIVER
                      (softly)
                   I'm sorry, son.

87   INT. A BAR SOMEWHERE. DAY.   87

       The bar seen earlier. A small group of PATRONS discuss
       developments. The WAITRESS seems upset, occasionally
       glancing to camera as she pours a beer.

                         PATRON 1
                   Why would he want to go to Chicago? Who
                   does he know from there?

                         PATRON 2
                   His doctor came from Chicago, didn't he?

                         PATRON 1
                   Wasn't his father from Chicago?

                         WAITRESS
                      (upset)
                   He's not going to Chicago. He's not going
                   anywhere. He has to have it out with Meryl.

88   EXT. STREET - TRUMAN'S BICYCLE. DAY.   88

       As TRUMAN rides home on his bicycle, he stares wildly about
       him - the rearview mirror on his bicycle is suddenly cause for
       concern, so are the trees and streetlamps lining the roadway.

89   EXT. TRUMAN'S BACKYARD. DAY.   89

       TRUMAN, staring at the highway from the bottom of the garden,
       doesn't bother to look up as MERYL, still wearing her nurse's
       uniform, approaches.

                         TRUMAN
                      (referring to a distant car on
                      the expressway)
                   See that car way down there? I bet it's
                   a Suburu station wagon.

       Meryl looks idly over the fence at the approaching car.
       Finally, a Suburu station wagon motors by. Meryl is
       unimpressed. Truman turns his back on the highway to
       continue his game.

                                                          (CONTINUED)

                    TRUMAN
          I predict the next four cars will be a
          white Honda Civic, a blue and white Dodge
          Dart with the front hubcap missing, a
          Volkswagon Beetle with a dented fender
          and a motorcycle.

Meryl doesn't wish to participate in the game and makes for
the house. Truman holds her arm, forcing her to watch. He
turns to check his prediction. A convoy of cars approaches.

                    TRUMAN
          There's the Honda...the Dodge...here
          comes the dented Beetle...

Meryl's attention wavers. Truman tightens his grip.

                    TRUMAN
          Look!

Following the VW is a school bus.

                    MERYL
               (mocking)
          Where's the motorcycle?

Truman is momentarily disappointed.

                    TRUMAN
          Don't you want to know how I did that?

A motorcycle putters by. Meryl turns and walks back to the
house. He hurries after her.

                    MERYL
          I invited Marlon and Rita for a barbeque
          Sunday. I thought I'd make my potato
          salad. Remind me--

                    TRUMAN
          I won't be here Sunday.

                    MERYL
          --we need more charcoal.

                    TRUMAN
          Are you listening to a word I'm saying?

                    MERYL
          You're upset because you want to go to
          Fiji. Is that it?

                                        (CONTINUED)

89   CONTINUED: (2)   89

Truman is puzzled by her conciliatory tone.

                    MERYL
          Okay, do it. Get it out of your system.
          Save for a few months and go. There.
          Happy now? I'm going to take a shower.

She turns away.

                    TRUMAN
               (catching her wrist)
          Let's go now.

                    MERYL
          What?!

Despite her protests, Truman drags Meryl towards his car.

                    TRUMAN
               (as he shoves her into the car)
          I'm ready to go now. Why wait?

90   INT. TRUMAN'S CAR. DAY.   90

TRUMAN holds MERYL's wrist to stop her exiting the car and
accelerates out of the driveway in reverse without looking -
almost running over PLUTO the dog and SPENCER with his
garbage can.

Truman starts circling a gazebo at the center of a
roundabout, faster and faster.

                    TRUMAN
          Where shall we go? Where shall we go?
          Spontaneity is what it's all about.
          Forget Fiji. We can't very well drive to
          Fiji, can we? What about Atlantic City?

                    MERYL
               (trying to mask her anxiety)
          You hate gambling.

                    TRUMAN
          That's right. I do, don't I?

                    MERYL
          So why do you want to go?

                    TRUMAN
          Because I never have. That's why you go
          places, isn't it?

                                                        (CONTINUED)

THE TRUMAN SHOW

TEXT BY ANDREW NICCOL

STILLS BY MELINDA SUE GORDON

Truman Burbank as himself. Before he could spell "celebrity" he was one—although for over twenty-nine years he had no inkling of his superstardom. Entire sections in bookstores and libraries are devoted to works analyzing the man and the phenomenon of "The Truman Show." His fans numbered in the billions. His show was beamed to over two hundred countries. More people tuned in to his first day of school than watched the presidential debates that year. In the twenty-fourth season, they had to reschedule the World Series so it wouldn't conflict with Truman's wedding. The ballplayers agreed it was the right thing to do.

Truman's delightful wife, "Meryl," played by Hannah Gill, was the pitchwoman on the show—since it ran 24 hours a day, there were no commercial breaks. Product placement was the only source of revenue. Hannah claimed that the constant hawking of merchandise—recipe books, fashion (The Meryl Line), housewares, and appliances— never affected her acting performance. She felt it was a matter of technique and that her earlier experience as a runway model had helped her achieve a subtlety in presentation.

Louis Coltrane, better known as "Marlon Lemmon," was a cast member since the age of eight. He suffered from a severe identity crisis, often claiming that it was he, not Truman, who was the real victim of the show (described in detail in his two books, *I, Marlon* and *Living A Part*). In the twenty-sixth season, Marlon found an advance synopsis that had him dying of brain cancer. He promptly confronted Christof, the show's creator, claiming, "This will kill Truman long before it kills me." Many believe it was a bluff on Christof's part since the incident occurred during contract negotiations. They settled on a benign tumor.

Walter Moore, who played Truman's father, "Kirk," hadn't bargained on how much he would bond with the boy. He was often criticized by director Christof for treating Truman as a son instead of a co-star. Kirk was conflicted about reining in a child who was a born explorer—and this ultimately led to his character being killed off in the "Drowning At Sea" episode. Guilt-ridden over the psychological impact the drowning had on Truman, Walter eventually snuck back onto the set disguised as an extra.

Alanis Montclair, who played "Mother," was one of the most influential characters in Truman's life. She faked nineteen major illnesses during the course of the show in an attempt to keep Truman in Seahaven, garnering several major awards in the process. She was almost definitely responsible for Truman entering the life insurance industry.

The enigmatic Christof, the show's conceiver, creator, director, and self-described "world's greatest televisionary." For a man who made his name invading Truman's privacy, Christof jealously guards his own personal life. There are unsubstantiated rumors of regular blood transfusions, that he sleeps in an all-white room, bathes in goat's milk, and that his true age is eighty-two. He has been in seclusion since the show's finale.

Downtown Seahaven. How many cameras can you spot? The entire set, the town and surrounding island of Seahaven, contained a myriad of hidden cameras, so compact and well-disguised they virtually defied detection. The system, designed by Christof, was called "OmniCam." All cameras were remote controlled, capable of recording sound, and had night-vision facility. Every person, vehicle, building, street lamp, bush, billboard, structure, protuberance, and cavity of any kind was camera-ready.

While the extras in Seahaven numbered only in the hundreds, imaginative use of wardrobe and make-up created the impression of a much larger population. The man on the bicycle in the foreground is Herbert Delaney, better known as "Mr. Forgettable" or "The Chameleon." Although he appeared in literally thousands of scenes with Truman, Truman never once recognized him.

One of the best-loved camera angles was the one concealed behind Truman's bathroom mirror. His morning monologues, often accompanied by soap drawings, are widely regarded as the best window into Truman's head and were some of the most popular segments in the show's history. These "Mirror Moments," as they came to be called, were packaged together on video and millions of copies sold worldwide.

As he leaves for work, Truman is greeted by Pluto, the next-door-neighbor's dog. Four identical Dalmatians played the role of "Pluto" throughout the years. One time, Pluto was actually played by a female named "Wanda." In the background is Ira Dorsett, who played Truman's next-door-neighbor, "Spencer." For eight seasons, Ira provided a valuable camera angle for the show from his unique Trashcan Cam —also known in the industry as the SpencerCam. Truman never questioned the continuity error that, for a man who lived alone, Spencer had an awful lot of garbage.

The moment that perhaps signaled the beginning of the end of "The Truman Show." The entire night sky over Seahaven was a gigantic man-made canopy containing thousands of halogen lamps masquerading as the constellations —the world's largest planetarium. Since Truman was a stargazer, authenticity was critical. Sirius (9 Canis Major) fell onto Truman's street that fateful morning when a gaffer was changing a burnt-out bulb. The gaffer later stated that when it happened, he had to be stopped from jumping right after it. The production hastily concocted a story that the light had fallen off a jet liner, but Truman never seemed completely convinced.

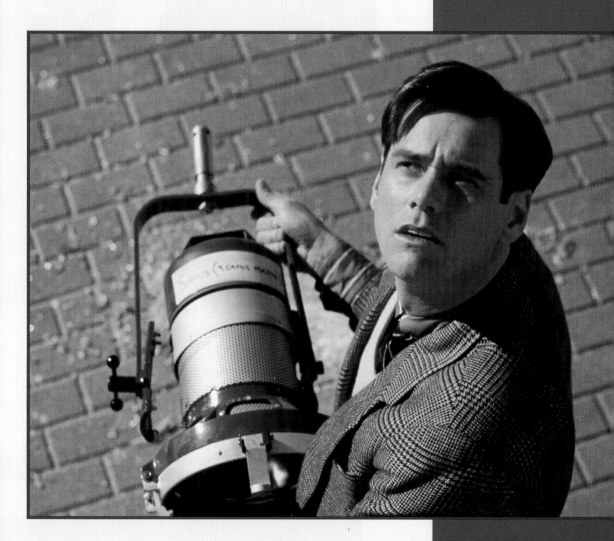

Monty Friedman, known to the TV public as "Errol," operated the most famous newsstand in the world. All of the magazines and newspapers were one-of-a-kind, customized props, since real periodicals would obviously be full of articles about Truman and "The Truman Show." In the nineteenth season, a copy of *Variety* was accidentally put on display with Truman's face on the front page. The world held its breath as Truman seemed to be reaching for it, but picked up a fashion magazine instead. Note the headline on the newspaper in this shot, extolling the virtues of Seahaven.

Instilling in Truman a fear of the water was Christof's most effective technique for keeping his leading man on the set. Twenty-two years after the "Drowning At Sea" episode, Truman was still unable to board the ferry to Harbor Island. A good thing too, since Harbor Island was merely a painted backdrop.

A cloud over Truman. Christof fired twenty-four Special Effects Supervisors during the course of the show, but admitted that authentic-looking rain was one effect that had always eluded him. Truman suspected nothing, since these "localized" rain showers were all he'd ever known. This, however, was of little consolation to Christof.

Christof insisted that Truman
had a healthy sex-life, but this
intimacy was handled very
tastefully with soft lighting and
classical music, often cutting
away to wind blowing in the
drapes. Hannah Gill would
carefully rehearse all of the
moves and angles with
Christof weeks in advance.
(Hannah often described her
feelings for her director as
"complicated.") In the days
before Truman's escape,
"Meryl" was desperately trying
to seduce Truman so that
the birth of their first child
would coincide with "Sweeps
Week" nine months later.

The one person in Truman's life who ever told him the truth, Sylvia was only an extra, never meant to have a speaking role. She actually forgot her character's name, "Lauren," when Truman approached her in the library—completely out of character for the timid young man. Many critics blamed Christof for the Sylvia incident, claiming she had a political agenda, was improperly screened, and inadequately coached. Christof took the biggest gamble in the show's history when he took so long to intervene. He later released a statement explaining that he wanted to reward Truman's boldness, but sources in the production claim that Christof realized it had been a major miscalculation.

Truman's attempts to re-create Sylvia's face were a source of constant embarrassment to Christof.

Like many cast members, Louis Coltrane became a multi-millionaire during his long-running role as a vending machine stockist and Truman's best friend. His endorsements included beer, clothing, golf equipment and, of course, The Marlon Bar—currently ranked number three in the world's confectionery market.

Another one of the psychological tricks used to keep Truman in Seahaven. The local travel agency encouraged Truman to do anything *but* travel. All of the holiday destinations looked suspiciously like Seahaven itself and posters pointed out the dangers of the world beyond this sheltered community: "*TRAVELERS BEWARE—Street Gangs, Disease, Wild Animals.*"

Truman unknowingly wore a camera himself for many years, concealed in his father's college ring. When he returned the ring to Kirk, accidentally, or deliberately, Truman gave himself a way to elude the production.

A prisoner in paradise? An aerial view of Truman in the uniquely designed suburb of Seahaven. Christof was concerned about what he called the "visual assault" taking place in modern architecture at the time the set was constructed. His brief to his production designers was a return to "modern classics"—he kept talking about a "human scale." Note the horizon. Looks real, doesn't it?

Although Christof, the show's director, often derided what he regarded as the overuse of pyrotechnics and special effects in modern television, he wasn't above using them himself when the need arose.

There have been dozens of documented attempts to "liberate" Truman. One of the most spectacular was the parachute jump from a lighting gantry in the twenty-eighth season by William Griffin, better known as "Billie Blackbird." Unfortunately for Billie, Truman turned his head at the critical moment and missed seeing the sign Billie was wearing—"TRUMAN, YOU'RE ON TV." The skydiver was quickly bundled out of sight. Billie later sued, claiming studio security guards tried to strangle him with his own rip cord, but a judge threw out the case stating, "If you try to jeopardize a major television show, there are consequences."

"Do something!" Much to Truman's horror, Meryl breaks the fourth wall and appeals to the production to intervene.

Truman's emotional reunion with Walter Moore, who played his father, "Kirk Burbank," until he was written out of the show in the eighth season. Walter later received an Emmy for this episode, awarded under controversial circumstances since Walter had admitted to the press that he had not been acting that evening, the emotion genuine.

Christof at his seat in the control room, also known as the "Lunar Room," 221 stories up in the OmniCam Ecosphere. The moon that Truman pondered his whole life was actually Christof's private window onto Seahaven.

The first prototype model of Seahaven that Christof presented to the studio heads— kept in the control room for inspiration. In fact, the final town was far larger.

Some insiders claim Christof's feelings for Truman were not those of a director for a star, but rather a father for a son. When asked on an episode of "Tru Talk" if he'd ever considered making a cameo appearance as a priest or a veterinarian, Christof responded that he didn't want to get emotionally involved.

Until Truman's escape on day 10,913, he had only been off-camera a total of forty-two minutes throughout his entire life. A technical fault in the twelfth season accounts for most of that time.

The control room where hundreds of operators covered every facet of Truman's life from every conceivable angle. Of course, Christof called the shots. One of the greatest creative challenges was shooting a sleeping subject—even more challenging before the advent of night-vision cameras in the twelfth season. Up until then, Truman was forced to sleep with a night light.

During critical moments in the show, global productivity would sharply decline as a worldwide audience tuned in. The show was especially popular in Taiwan, where there have been a number of copycat productions, including the short-lived, but highly graphic, "Me Ling: A Life."

Many viewers cared more about Truman than members of their own families. The woman on the right, Muriel Obernath, named all three of her sons after Truman and later abandoned her biological children when none proved as entertaining as the television child she had "adopted."

Roland Lyman, a celebrity in his own right, claimed to have watched every second of the twenty-nine-year-old show. Since "The Truman Show" ran twenty-four hours a day, Lyman, who averaged three hours of sleep per night, would later watch whatever he missed on tape. Lyman died tragically of electrocution during the show's final minutes when his television set fell into the bathtub.

Truman finally discovers the confines of his world.

The ocean that Truman had feared for most of his life was actually a tank containing over six hundred and fifty million gallons of synthetic salt water, temperature controlled. The sky, a cyclorama made of a polymer fabric, was developed by the space program. The "Truman Stage" is one of only two man-made structures visible from space—the other being the more diminutive Great Wall of China.

The last image seen by viewers before transmission was cut and "The Truman Show" went off the air forever. (Of course, the studio does have almost thirty years worth of re-runs.)

                      MERYL
        Truman, I think I'm going to throw up.

Truman roars off down the street.

                     TRUMAN
        Me too.

Almost immediately, Truman encounters a traffic snarl.

                     TRUMAN
         (a manic edge to his voice)
        So much traffic, this time of day. Does
        that strike you as peculiar?

Without warning, Truman suddenly dives down a sidestreet. But
his move is anticipated. At the end of the street, a pack of
cars suddenly appears. Other vehicles fill the gap behind.

                     TRUMAN
         (to Meryl, marveling)
        Blocked at every turn. Beautifully
        synchronized, don't you agree?

                     MERYL
         (incredulous)
        You blaming me for the traffic?

                     TRUMAN
        Should I?

Truman reverses suddenly and makes a U-turn.

                     TRUMAN
        You're right. We could be stuck here
        for hours. Could be like this all
        the way to Atlantic City. Let's go
        back. I'm sorry. I don't know what
        got into me.

Truman starts heading back the way they came, the roadway now
relatively free of traffic.

                     MERYL
        Would you please slow down, Truman?

Truman floors the car. The car flies past their house.

                     MERYL
        Truman, that was our house!

(CONTINUED)

90   CONTINUED: (2)   90

                              TRUMAN
                    I've changed my mind again. What's New
                    Orleans like this time of year? Mardi
                    Gras. Or let's just see where the road
                    takes us.

                              MERYL
                         (pleading)
                    Let me out, Truman. You're not right in
                    the head. You want to destroy yourself,
                    you do it on your own!

                              TRUMAN
                         (eerily calm)
                    I think I'd like a little company.

          As he speeds erratically, Truman glances at the streets on
          either side of the main road where he discovers a distinct
          lack of moving traffic.

                              TRUMAN
                         (to the anxious Meryl at his side)
                    Look, Meryl. No cars! I don't run into
                    traffic. The traffic follows me around.
                         (excited by his discovery)
                    We're in a moving pack, don't you see?

91   INT/EXT. TRUMAN'S CAR - BRIDGE. DAY.   91

          But TRUMAN's clear path is short-lived. He is forced to slow
          once again behind a line of other cars at a bridge.

                              TRUMAN
                         (to Meryl)
                    It's hard to go places, isn't it?

                              MERYL
                         (looking up ahead at an
                         overturned car)
                    There's been an accident, Truman.

                              TRUMAN
                    Uhuh. There's no accident. It's just
                    more stalling.

          Truman floors the car again and swerves into the oncoming
          lane. He roars along the bridge on the wrong side of the
          road. Near the end of the bridge, a distraught MOTORIST
          dashes into the middle of the road, waving his arms. Truman
          slams on the brakes.

                                                            (CONTINUED)

91   CONTINUED: 91

                              MOTORIST
                    (pointing to a small BOY lying
                    very still on the ground
                    beside a wrecked car)
              --is there a doctor, a nurse?

                              MERYL
              Truman, it's a child. I've got to help -

                              TRUMAN
                    (hardly glancing to the boy)
              He'll be fine.

Truman roars on, almost bowling over the concerned motorist.

                              MERYL
              Truman, I took the "hypocrite" oath!

                              TRUMAN
              I bet you did.

Truman roars past a sign that reads, *"YOU ARE NOW LEAVING
SEAHAVEN - Are you sure that's a good idea?"*

Back at the accident scene, the little boy, apparently
uninjured, sits up.

92   INT/EXT. CAR. DAY.   92

They roar pass an illuminated sign - *"FOREST FIRE WARNING -
Extreme Danger"*.

                              MERYL
              Truman, what about that sign?

                              TRUMAN
              I'm sure they're just exaggerating.

Suddenly, a 20 foot high wall of flame shoots across the
roadway in front of them - as if someone flicked on a gas
switch.

                              MERYL
              What about that - do you believe *that*?!

TRUMAN experiences his first moment of doubt. He looks to
the terrified MERYL, then closes his eyes tightly and
accelerates through the fire wall. He is startled to find
that they have emerged on the other side, singed but
unscathed.

                                                        (CONTINUED)

92   CONTINUED: 92

However, the open road in front of them now disturbs Truman
for a different reason - its sheer lack of anything unusual.
Signs along the road advertise motels and give directions to
other destinations - *"I-6211 - 2 miles"*, *"Notel Motel - Pool,
Color TV"*.

Meryl also now appears to be resigned to the journey.

                    MERYL
          So what do we do for money when we get to
          New Orleans?

                    TRUMAN
               (not so confident now)
          I've got my Seahaven Bankcard.

                    MERYL
          So we just eat into our savings, is that
          the idea? I'd better call your mother
          when we get there. She'll be worried
          sick - I don't know how she's going to
          take this.

Truman appears very unsure of himself.

93   EXT. ROADWAY. DAY.   93

However, there is still a barrier between TRUMAN and Bourbon
Street. The highway, leading to a cloverleaf freeway
junction in the distance, is completely blocked off by
Seahaven police cars. No way past. Nuclear silos in the
distance spew out an ominous puff of smoke. A sign reads,
*"SEAHAVEN ISLAND NUCLEAR POWER STATION - Clean, Safe,
Economical - More Power To You!"*

Truman is forced to slow at the police barricade.

                    TRUMAN
          Now what?

                    OFFICER
               (grim-faced, indicating the
               nearby power plant)
          Leak at the plant. They had to shut
          her down.

                    TRUMAN
          Is there any way around?

                    OFFICER
          The whole area's being evacuated.

                                                        (CONTINUED)

93   CONTINUED: 93

                         TRUMAN
             Well, thank you for your help.

                         OFFICER
             You're welcome, Truman.

Truman's eyes widen at the mention of his name from an
apparent stranger. As the officer turns, Truman bolts from
the car, leaving MERYL in the passenger seat.

                         MERYL
                Truman!! Come back!!

Truman flees into the forest.

94   INT. A LIVING ROOM SOMEWHERE. DAY.   94

The TWO OLD LADIES we have observed before are almost overcome
with tension. One lady reaches out for her companion's hand.

95   EXT.   FOREST NEAR SEAHAVEN NUCLEAR POWER PLANT. DAY.   95

TRUMAN bursts past the alien-looking HAZARDOUS WASTE WORKERS
in their protective suits carrying detection instruments.
The workers give chase in their cumbersome suits, trying to
cut off his path.

Nearing the edge of the forest, Truman hears the sound of
hammers and saws. But before he has time to see the source
of the sound, he is tackled to the ground.

As SEAHAVEN POLICE OFFICERS drag him away, one of the WASTE
WORKERS walks the remaining few yards, pushing aside a wall
of tropical foliage. We now see what Truman was prevented
from seeing.

A Polynesian island is under construction by dozens of
RIGGERS, PAINTERS and SET DECORATORS. Large cranes are
lifting palm trees into place, a fake volcano is being tested
in the distance and rehearsals for a firewalking ceremony are
underway complete with hot coals, DRUMMERS and FIREWALKERS in
native dress.

The wings and fuselage of an airliner are being constructed
on a hydraulic gimbal. Leading into one side of the airliner
is a covered walkway, emblazoned with a sign, *"Seahaven
Island - Departures"*. Emerging from the opposite side of the
airliner is an old-fashioned airline stairway with the sign,
"Welcome To Fiji".

At the foot of the steps, TWO WOMEN in Fijian dress are being
shown the correct way to present a floral lei.

                                              (CONTINUED)

95   CONTINUED: 95

                         FIJIAN WOMAN
              Did he see us?

                         WASTE WORKER
                    (into microphone)
              Negative.

96   INT. TRUMAN'S HOUSE - KITCHEN. NIGHT.   96

MERYL shows TWO SEAHAVEN POLICEMEN out the back door.

                         MERYL
              Thank you.

                         POLICEMAN 1
              You're lucky he's not glowing, Ma'am.
              Next time we'll have to file charges.

Meryl joins TRUMAN at the kitchen table. Truman applauds
ironically.

                         MERYL
              Let me get you some help, Truman. You're
              not well.

                         TRUMAN
                    (ignoring her medical advice)
              Why do you want to have a child with me?
              You can't stand me.

                         MERYL
              That's not true.

Meryl picks up a package and holds it to camera.

                         MERYL
              Why don't I make you some of this new
              Mococoa Drink? All natural. Cocoa beans
              from the upper slopes of Mount Nicaragua.
              No artificial sweeteners--

                         TRUMAN
                    (incredulous)
              --What the hell are you talking about?!

                         MERYL
              I've tasted other cocoas. This is the best.

Truman rises from the table and backs her around the room.

                                                    (CONTINUED)

                         TRUMAN
           What the hell has that got to do with
           anything? Tell me what's happening?!

                         MERYL
                   (frightened but remaining
                   poised)
           You're having a nervous breakdown, that's
           what's happening.

                         TRUMAN
                   (backing her up against the
                   kitchen bench)
           You're part of this, aren't you?!

     Meryl grabs the "Chef's-Mate" from the counter to protect
     herself. She points the potato peeler at him.

                         MERYL
           Truman, you're scaring me!

     Truman looks into her eyes and, with surprising swiftness,
     grabs her wrist and disarms her.

                         TRUMAN
           No, you're scaring me, Meryl!

     Truman grabs Meryl and turns the Chef's Mate on her. He
     stares wildly about him.

                         TRUMAN
           Stop this now. I'll do it. I swear.

                         MERYL
           Do something...

     Upon hearing her remark, Truman's eyes widen. Sensing that
     she too is addressing a third person, he jerks her head
     around to read her face.

                         TRUMAN
                   (wild-eyed)
           Who were you talking to?!

                         MERYL
                   (incredulous)
           You're the one talking to the walls!

                         TRUMAN
           No. You said, "Do something." Who were
           you talking to? Tell me!

(CONTINUED)

96   CONTINUED: (2)   96

                         MERYL
               Truman, stop it!

Suddenly, the front door chimes.

                         TRUMAN
               Right on time. Cops must be telepathic.

Truman grabs his peeler and marches Meryl down the hallway to
the front door. The doorbell chimes a second and third time,
more insistently.

                         TRUMAN
                    (shouting through the closed door)
               Stay where you are!

                         MARLON (O.C.)
               Truman? It's me, Marlon. I need to talk
               to you.

Truman flinches. He was so convinced it would be the police.
He takes a step back against the hallway wall. Before he can
decide what to do, MARLON has opened the unlocked front door
to be confronted with the sight of Truman holding the peeler
to Meryl's throat.

Marlon locks eyes with Truman. Sizing up the situation, he
slowly but decisively removes the peeler from Truman's hand.
Meryl wrenches herself free from Truman's now limp grasp and
collapses into Marlon's arms, sobbing.

                         MERYL
                    (distraught)
               How can anyone expect me to carry on
               under these conditions? This
               is...*unprofessional*.

97   EXT. UNFINISHED BRIDGE. NIGHT.   97

MARLON and TRUMAN, both nursing bottles of beer, sit on the
end of the unfinished bridge.

                         TRUMAN
               I don't know what to think, Marlon.
               Maybe I'm going out of my mind, but I
               get the feeling that the world revolves
               around me somehow.

                         MARLON
               It's a lot of world for one man. You sure
               that's not wishful thinking, you wishing
               you'd made something more of yourself?
                    (MORE)

                                                          (CONTINUED)

97   CONTINUED: 97

                    MARLON (cont'd)
          Christ, Truman, who hasn't sat on the John
          and had an imaginary interview on
          "Seahaven Tonight"?   Who hasn't wanted to
          be somebody?

                    TRUMAN
          This is different. Everybody seems to be
          in on it.

Marlon looks around as if drawing inspiration from somewhere
in the night.

                    MARLON
          Tru, we've known each other since before
          we were in long pants. The only way we
          ever made it through high school was
          cheating off each other's test papers.
          Jesus, they were identical. I always
          liked that, because whatever the answer
          was--

Truman chimes in, nodding fondly at the memory.

                    TRUMAN & MARLON
          --we were right together and we were
          wrong together.

                    MARLON
          The only night either of us ever spent
          in jail, we spent together and I wet
          myself but you never told anyone. I was
          best man at your wedding and my brother
          was best man at my wedding and you didn't
          talk to me for a month over that and I
          didn't blame you because you've been more
          of a brother to me than he's ever been.

Truman is slowly coming around - Marlon's speech from the
heart soothing away his pain.

                    MARLON
          I know things haven't worked out for
          either of us like we used to sit up on
          Monroe Avenue all night and dream they
          would. We all let opportunities pass us
          by. None of us asks for the dance as
          often as we should. I know that feeling
          when it's like everything's slipping away
          and you don't want to believe it so you
          look for answers someplace else. But,
          well, the point is, I would gladly step
          in front of traffic for you.

98   INT.   CONTROL ROOM.   NIGHT.   98

CHRISTOF stares intently into camera, holding his distinctive
earpiece to his head. Beside him, his ever-present assistant,
CHLOE.

>   CHRISTOF
>   (hushed tones)
>   And the last thing I'd ever do is lie
>   to you.

99   EXT.   FREEWAY.   NIGHT.   99

>   MARLON
>   (staring into Truman's eyes)
>   And the last thing I'd ever do is lie to you.
>   (pause)
>   Think about it, Truman, if everybody's
>   in on it, I'd have to be in on it too.
>   I'm not in on it, because there is no *it*.

>   TRUMAN
>   So what are you saying, Marlon, the whole
>   thing has been in my head--?

>   MARLON
>   (meeting his gaze)
>   Not the *whole* thing, Truman. You were
>   right about *one* thing.

>   TRUMAN
>   What's that?

>   MARLON
>   The thing that started all of this.

TRUMAN looks up in the direction of MARLON's gaze. A FIGURE
stands at the end of the freeway - a homeless man. It is his
father, KIRK.

>   MARLON
>   Yes, he survived somehow. He's got quite a
>   story to tell.

Marlon helps Truman to his feet - Truman still transfixed by
the figure.

>   MARLON
>   Go to him.

100   INT.   CONTROL ROOM.   NIGHT.   100

CHRISTOF continues to direct the action from what is now
revealed to be the control room of a television studio.

                    CHRISTOF
          Go wide, LightCam Eight...

In a wide shot, from one of the streetlights lining the
empty freeway, we see TRUMAN walking towards his long lost
FATHER.

                    CHRISTOF
          ...CurbCam Twelve...*and*...cue
          music...Beethoven, Third Symphony, Second
          Movement.

Music swells. Kirk and Truman embrace in the middle of the
freeway. Truman takes his father's ring from his own
finger.

                    CHRISTOF
          ...RingCam...

We see a close up of Kirk from the ring's POV. Truman places
the ring in the palm of his father's hand.

                    CHRISTOF
          ...ButtonCam Three...

We see a close up of Truman from a camera on Kirk's coat.

                    TRUMAN
          I never stopped believing.

                    KIRK
               (gazing at the ring, then up
               to Truman's face)
          Thank you...my son.

                    CHRISTOF
          And wide...

SIMEON looks to his director.

                    SIMEON
          Close up?

                    CHRISTOF
               (staring intently at his
               monitor)
          No, hold back...

                                                        (CONTINUED)

100   CONTINUED: 100

The CREW watches Kirk and Truman embrace.

                        KIRK
            All those years, wasted.

                        TRUMAN
            We have a lot of years ahead.

101   INT. CONTROL ROOM. NIGHT.   101

CHRISTOF allows himself a smile of satisfaction.

                        CHRISTOF
            And fade up music...*now* go in close...

As a tight two-shot of father and son fills the screen, the
orchestra swells with triumphant music.

102   EXT. FREEWAY. NIGHT.   102

FATHER and SON remain in the embrace. Over Truman's shoulder,
we see a flash of guilt flicker across MARLON's face.

103   INT. CONTROL ROOM. NIGHT.   103

CHRISTOF, emotionally drained by the events, slumps in his
chair. CHLOE rests a supportive hand on his shoulder. The head
of the network, MOSES, a man in his seventies, enters with his
young assistant, ROMAN - their faces full of admiration.

                        MOSES
            Well done. Well done, everyone.

104   INT. A BEDROOM SOMEWHERE. NIGHT.   104

A YOUNG WOMAN reclines on a bed, her back against the wall.
Propped up on her knees is a book. However, she's not
reading but staring straight into camera - a look of profound
sadness on her face. It is SYLVIA.

From her point-of-view, we see a portable television set on a
table at the foot of the bed.

On the television is a live picture of TRUMAN - the first
time we have seen him on a television screen. He is sitting
at his kitchen table, unaware of the cameras recording him.

The shot is static. He just sits there in silence, a
steaming cup of cocoa in front of him and a plate of
untouched cookies.

                                                    (CONTINUED)

At one point, a sponsor's border appears on the screen,
tastefully framing the "action", with the message, *"MOCOCOA -
Cocoa beans from the upper slopes of Mount Nicaragua"*. After
several seconds the border disappears.

Suddenly, the live picture of Truman shrinks into a window on
the screen to accommodate a title sequence that begins to
play around the edge of the image. "The Truman Show" theme
music begins.

The camera cranes up and over the Hollywood sign, the
flatlands of Burbank stretching into the distance.

                    ANNOUNCER (VO)
               From the network that never sleeps -
               broadcasting live and unedited 24 hours a
               day, 7 days a week, around the globe...

During this continuous aerial shot, overlapping scenes from
Truman's life appear in chronological order, from infancy to
adolescence and finally adulthood. Photographs of leading
CAST MEMBERS also appear in individual frames.

                    ANNOUNCER (VO)
               ...with Hannah Gill as Meryl Burbank,
               Louis Coltrane as Marlon, Alanis Montclair
               as Mother, re-introducing Walter Moore as
               her husband, Kirk...

The music swells as the camera approaches a mammoth structure at
the base of the mountains - a dome so vast it dwarfs everything
around it. At the top of the dome is a huge painting of Truman's
face encircled by satellite dishes - inside each dish is a single
letter spelling out, T-H-E T-R-U-M-A-N S-H-O-W - a banner
proclaims, *"30th Great Year"*.

                    ANNOUNCER (VO)
               ...and Truman Burbank as Himself, taped
               in the world's largest studio, one of
               only two man-made structures visible from
               space, comes the longest running
               documentary soap opera in history, now in
               its 30th great year - *"The Truman Show"*!

The camera rushes towards the outside wall of the gigantic dome
bathed in sunlight. When we emerge on the other side, it is
night. The camera cranes up from a calm, moonlit ocean to the
nightsky above. As we near the crescent-shaped moon, we
discover that it is actually a window overlooking Seahaven.
Standing in the "crater" window is the suited CHRISTOF.

105   INT. LUNAR STUDIO. NIGHT.   105

Pulling back from the window we reveal an INTERVIEWER, mid-
forties, conservative suit and hair. A large television
shows a live picture of Truman, immersed in his book.

>   INTERVIEWER
>   I'm your host, Mike Michaelson, coming to
>   you live from the Lunar Room on the 121st
>   story of the OmniCam Ecosphere, 2800 feet
>   above Seahaven Island. Tonight, a
>   special edition of "Tru Talk", the forum
>   where we discuss and analyze recent
>   events on the show. We are honored to
>   bring you a rare and exclusive interview
>   with the show's conceiver, creator, tele-
>   visionary, the Man-In-The-Moon himself--
>   Christof.
>   (referring to the image of
>   Truman between them)
>   I remind viewers that as "The Truman Show" is
>   a living history, it is our practice to keep
>   the image of Truman on screen at all times.

A TITLE APPEARS: *Due to the live and unedited nature of the
program, viewer discretion is advised.*

The Interviewer turns to Christof.

>   INTERVIEWER
>   Welcome.

>   CHRISTOF
>   Thank you.

>   INTERVIEWER
>   The catalyst for the recent dramatic
>   events was of course Truman's father,
>   Kirk, and his infiltration onto the show.
>   Before we discuss that, it's worth
>   reminding viewers that this isn't the
>   first time someone from the outside world
>   has tried to reach Truman.

>   CHRISTOF
>   We *have* had our close calls in the past.

Behind the two men, the constantly playing image of Truman
engrossed in his book is relegated to a window on the screen.

106   *PLAYBACK* - INT.   TRUMAN'S HOME.   CHRISTMAS MORNING.   106

    TRUMAN, 7, is opening presents under the tree - KIRK and
MOTHER proudly looking on.

                    INTERVIEWER
          Who can forget the infamous "Christmas
          Present" incident in the seventh season?

    Suddenly, a small MAN bursts from a large, Christmas parcel.
Kirk and the man grapple on the floor in front of the stunned
seven-year-old. Kirk drags him away.

107   *PLAYBACK* - EXT.   CITY STREET.   DAY.   107

    As the adult TRUMAN makes his way to work, a PARACHUTIST drops
from the sky into the main street, only yards behind him.

                    INTERVIEWER
          And only last summer "Billie Blackbird"
          made his third attempt, leaping from a
          lighting gantry.

    The parachutist is dressed entirely in black with a message
emblazoned on his chest, *"TRUMAN, YOU'RE ON TV."* COMMUTERS
grab the man and drag him away - Truman blissfully unaware of
the incident.

                    CHRISTOF
          (dismissive)
          These people have their own agendas.
          Many just want to be on television
          themselves.

108   *PLAYBACK* - EXT.   CITY STREET.   DAY.   108

    The encounter between TRUMAN and the homeless KIRK is
replayed up to the point where Kirk is bundled onto the bus.

                    INTERVIEWER
          Of course, there has never been anything
          to compare with this - the first time an
          intruder has been a former cast member--

                    CHRISTOF
          --a dead one at that.

                    INTERVIEWER
          --and certainly the first time that an
          intruder has been rewarded with a
          starring role.
          (MORE)

(CONTINUED)

108 CONTINUED: 108

>   INTERVIEWER (cont'd)
>   (gushing)
>   I really must congratulate you on writing
>   Kirk back in. A master stroke.
>
>   CHRISTOF
>   (feigning modesty)
>   Since Kirk started this whole crisis in
>   Truman's life, I came to the conclusion
>   that he was the only one who could end it.
>
>   INTERVIEWER
>   I understand he's hardly had a life of
>   his own since he left the show. How did
>   you convince him--was it the opportunity
>   to be close to Truman again?
>
>   CHRISTOF
>   That and a fat, new contract.
>
>   INTERVIEWER
>   How *do* you intend to explain his twenty-
>   two year absence?
>
>   CHRISTOF
>   Amnesia.
>
>   INTERVIEWER
>   (impressed, nodding in
>   agreement)
>   Of course.

The Interviewer consults his notes.

>   INTERVIEWER
>   Let's talk ratings. "Truman" has always
>   enjoyed top ten status but the huge surge
>   over the last few days--how do you hope
>   to sustain that audience now that Truman
>   appears to have reconciled himself?
>
>   CHRISTOF
>   As you know ratings have never been our
>   primary goal. I imagine we'll lose those
>   voyeurs only interested in witnessing
>   Truman's latest torment. However, I'm
>   certain that our core audience will
>   remain loyal.
>
>   INTERVIEWER
>   But recent events have been so dramatic,
>   it does raise the perennial question.
>   What keeps us watching this one man
>   twenty-four hours a day - eating,
>   (MORE)

                                              (CONTINUED)

108   CONTINUED: (2)   108

                        INTERVIEWER (cont'd)
           sleeping, working, sitting for hours in
           contemplation?

                        CHRISTOF
           It has to be the reality.

During this segment, we cut to a cross-section of VIEWERS -
the WAITRESS and BARMAN in the bar, the TWO OLD WOMEN on
their sofa, the TWO SECURITY GUARDS and the MAN in the bath -
listening to Christof's theories on their viewing habits.

                        CHRISTOF
           We've become tired of watching actors give
           us phony emotions, bored with pyrotechnics
           and special effects. While the world he
           inhabits is counterfeit, there's nothing
           fake about Truman himself. No scripts, no
           cue cards. It's not always Shakespeare
           but it's genuine. That's how he can
           support an entire channel.

                        INTERVIEWER
           A window onto the human condition?

                        CHRISTOF
           I prefer to think of it as a mirror.

At that moment, Truman - still live on the screen -
unwittingly punctuates the pretentious remark with a belch.
Christof and the Interviewer try not to notice.

                        CHRISTOF
           Not only does he give us a glimpse of the
           truth, he gives us a glimpse of ourselves.

                        INTERVIEWER
           But how do you account for the popularity of
           those eight hours a day when Truman sleeps?

                        CHRISTOF
           We find many viewers leave him on all
           night for comfort. Haven't you ever
           watched your child or your lover sleep?

                        INTERVIEWER
           Let's go to some of those viewers' calls.

The Interviewer presses a blinking, illuminated button on his
desk's high-tech phone terminal. During this segment,
various windows open on the screen advertising products from
the "Truman" catalogue.

                                       (CONTINUED)

> INTERVIEWER
Charlotte, North Carolina, for Christof.

> MALE CALLER 1
> (O.S.)
> (filtered, from speaker phone)
Hello?

> INTERVIEWER
You're on, Caller. Go ahead.

> MALE CALLER 1
Christof, it's a great honor to speak
with you.

> CHRISTOF
Thank you.

> MALE CALLER 1
How much of a strain has the last few
days placed on the actors?

> CHRISTOF
Working on "Truman" has always been a
huge commitment for an actor, not just in
terms of separation from friends and
family, but since Truman essentially
drives the plot, it is a never-ending
improvisation - witness Marlon's
extraordinary performance in the recent
"Father And Son Reunion" episode.

> INTERVIEWER
> (cutting off the call)
Are we talking Emmies?

> CHRISTOF
Certainly a nomination.

> INTERVIEWER
Of course, Truman has always been very
much in on casting.

> CHRISTOF
As with our own lives, the only people he
can't cast are his family. Otherwise he
has final approval, able to elevate an
extra into a lead role as was the case
with his only real friend, Marlon, or
alternatively relegate a star to a bit
player.

(CONTINUED)

                    INTERVIEWER
               (pressing another line)
          Istanbul, Turkey, you're on with master
          videographer, Christof.

                    FEMALE CALLER 1
                    (O.C.)
          Christof, I've admired your work my whole
          life, although I can't say I've seen it all.

                    CHRISTOF
          Who can?

                    FEMALE CALLER 1
          Can you settle an argument for me?
          What's the longest time Truman has been
          off-camera?

                    CHRISTOF
               (trace of pride)
          In his entire life, forty-two minutes. A
          technical fault in the twelfth season
          accounts for most of that time. The
          remainder generally results from
          blindspots, in the early days, when
          Truman would stray out of range of our
          cameras.

                    INTERVIEWER
          We should remind viewers that Truman,
          especially as a child, presented a
          challenge for the production.

                    CHRISTOF
               (turning to the screen)
          Let me demonstrate with some examples.

          Footage of TRUMAN as a baby appears on the screen - as a
          newborn INFANT, held in a pair of anonymous latex-gloved
          hands, and as a TODDLER, dressed in various baby outfits - on
          one occasion looking through the bars of his crib.

                    CHRISTOF
          He was curious from birth - premature by
          two weeks, as if he couldn't wait to get
          started.

                    INTERVIEWER
          Of course, his eagerness to leave his
          mother's womb also meant he was the one
          selected.

                          CHRISTOF
                     (enthusing)
          In competition with five other unwanted
          pregnancies - the casting of a show
          determined by an air date - he was the
          one who arrived on cue.

                          INTERVIEWER
          Who knew that a show originally meant to
          last one year - "Bringing Up Baby" -
          would turn into a "cradle to grave"
          concept. He is in fact the first child
          in the world to be legally adopted by a
          corporation.

                          CHRISTOF
          That's correct.

                          INTERVIEWER
          And the show now generates a yearly
          income equivalent to the gross national
          product of a small country.

                          CHRISTOF
          People forget it takes the *population* of
          an entire country to keep the show
          running.

                          INTERVIEWER
          I believe your own shareholding in
          OmniCam is in the order of--

                          CHRISTOF
          --Why is an artist plagued with these
          questions? I've never done this for any
          monetary gain.

                          INTERVIEWER
          No, of course not.
                     (quickly changing the subject)
          And since the show runs 24 hours a day
          with no commercial breaks the staggering
          profits are all generated from product
          placement.

                          CHRISTOF
          Yes, everything you see on the show is
          for sale - from the actors' wardrobe,
          food products, to the very homes they
          live in--

                                            (CONTINUED)

108   CONTINUED: (6)   108

                    INTERVIEWER
          All products carefully chosen and
          tested by you for quality and
          aesthetic value.

                    CHRISTOF
          There's nothing on the show I don't
          use myself.

                    INTERVIEWER
          And it's all available in the "Truman
          Show" catalogue. Operators are
          standing by.

Christof nods.

                    INTERVIEWER
          Why do you feel that Truman's never
          come close to discovering the true
          nature of his world?

                    CHRISTOF
          We accept the reality of the world with
          which we're presented. As the show
          expanded, naturally we were forced to
          manufacture ways to keep Truman in
          Seahaven - demonstrating that every
          venture is accompanied by a risk.

The SEVEN-YEAR-OLD TRUMAN we have seen in other flashbacks
appears on the screen. Wearing a cowboy outfit, he goes to
cross the walkway of a bridge when he is suddenly confronted
by a savage DOG wearing a spiked collar.

                    CHRISTOF
          Later, Kirk's drowning made much of
          this kind of intervention unnecessary.

We freeze on seven-year old Truman's terrified face.

                    INTERVIEWER
          You've never actually met Truman,
          yourself. Never thought about doing a
          cameo -- playing a veterinarian, or a
          priest, something like that?

                    CHRISTOF
          I've been tempted. But I think it's
          important to retain objectivity. I
          wouldn't want to get emotionally
          caught up.

                                        (CONTINUED)

>   INTERVIEWER
>   The Hague for Christof...The
>   Hague?...lost them.
>   (pressing another line)
>   Hollywood, California, you're on "Tru Talk".

>   FEMALE CALLER 2 (O.S.)
>   How can you say he lives a life like
>   any other?

>   CHRISTOF
>   (sensing the thinly
>   disguised resentment in the
>   Caller's voice)
>   As the Bard says, "All the world's a
>   stage, and all the men and women merely
>   players." The only difference between
>   Truman and ourselves is that his life is
>   more thoroughly documented. He is
>   confronted with the same obstacles and
>   influences that confront us all. He
>   plays his allotted roles as we all do--

>   FEMALE CALLER 2
>   --He's not a performer. He's a prisoner.

The Interviewer goes to cut off the call, but Christof stops him.

>   CHRISTOF
>   (rising to the challenge)
>   And can you tell me, caller, that you're
>   not a player on the stage of life -
>   playing out your allotted role? He can
>   leave at any time. If his was more than
>   just a vague ambition, if he were
>   absolutely determined to discover the
>   truth, there's no way we could prevent
>   him. I think what really distresses you,
>   Caller, is that ultimately Truman prefers
>   the comfort of his "cell" as you call it.

>   FEMALE CALLER 2
>   (as if trying to convince
>   herself, giving herself away)
>   --No, you're wrong! He'll prove you
>   wrong! He can still do it!

The Interviewer hangs up on the caller.

109   INT.   A BEDROOM SOMEWHERE.   NIGHT.   109

In a darkly lit room, we see SYLVIA.   It is she who is the
confrontational Caller - phone still in her hand.

                    CHRISTOF
                (from the television)
        We've learnt about life as Truman has
        and, despite the complaints of a
        minority, it's been an overwhelmingly
        positive experience, for Truman and for
        the viewing public.

                    INTERVIEWER
        Let's take another call.
                (pressing a line)
        London, England you're on "Tru Talk".

                    MALE CALLER 2
                    (O.S.)
        Christof? Congratulations on the way you've
        always handled Truman's "sex" life - the
        classical music, soft lighting and so on.
        But has the recent violence caused a problem
        for the show's sponsors?

                    CHRISTOF
        The sponsors know the risks going in,
        although we do try to maintain standards
        - a level of decorum. For instance, I've
        never put a camera in the toilet.

Still in silhouette, SYLVIA turns down the volume on the
television. Focusing on the window on the screen that
displays TRUMAN, she comes close to the screen, catching his
melancholy, saddened by his regression.

109A INT.   TRUMAN'S BASEMENT.   MORNING.   109A

TRUMAN breathes in the scent of Sylvia's sweater one last
time before reluctantly replacing it in the trunk, together
with his book, *"To The Ends Of The Earth - The Age Of
Exploration"*. For a final time, he regards his unfinished
picture of SYLVIA inside - two holes where the eyes should
be. As he does so, he finds two lost paper cuttings - a pair
of eyes on the basement floor. He tries them. Ironically
they fit - the picture completed. He closes the trunk
anyway. With a sense of finality, he fastens the lock.

110   INT. CONTROL ROOM. NIGHT.   110

The giant ON-AIR monitor in the control room plays a closeup
shot of Truman sleeping.

CHRISTOF comes close to the monitor and almost touches the
screen. As he does so, Truman twitches in his sleep.

111   INT. BATHROOM. MORNING.   111

TRUMAN wipes the mist from the mirror of the bathroom cabinet
and stares into it in a way he has never done before.

111A INT. CONTROL ROOM. MORNING.   111A

Close up on the giant ON-AIR monitor in the control room.
It displays a wide shot of Truman staring into the bathroom
mirror.

We slowly pull back to reveal SIMEON and the other VIDEO
OPERATORS sitting at the mixing desks arranged in tiers
reminiscent of an auditorium or NASA's Mission Control.
Each mixing desk contains a dozen-or-so built-in monitors
and is designated with a location such as *Truman's House
- Interior*, *Truman's Office - Cubicle*, *Tyrone's Deli*.
The operator at each desk, sitting in a swivel chair and
wearing the slimmest of heatsets, is responsible for
monitoring a particular location.

The monitors cover virtually every facet of Truman's life.
Camera angles from the interior of Truman's house, his
backyard, car, office, the deli he frequents, the seashore
to which he is drawn, the unfinished bridge where he golfs
with Marlon - many of the locations strangely devoid of
people.

Simeon, seated in the front row of mixing desks, stares back
at Truman's image on the monitor, slightly unnerved.

                    SIMEON
              (to a nearby COLLEAGUE)
           Is he looking at us?

As if to reassure the technician, Truman begins one of his
familiar monologues. He talks to the mirror as if being
interviewed.

                    TRUMAN
           --What are my plans now? Well, next I'm
           thinking of tackling the Yuba River in an
           authentic canoe from the Algonquin tribe.
                    (MORE)

                                                    (CONTINUED)

111A CONTINUED: 111A

                         TRUMAN (cont'd)
          -- I'm talking about the north fork, a
          class five rapid - only I'm not going
          down the Yuba, I'm going *up*. Do you
          honestly think for one minute I'd go back
          to some dreary office to rubber stamp
          meaningless documents...do you?

                         MERYL (O.C.)
          --Truman, you're gonna be late!

     Truman sighs as he exits the bathroom.

112 EXT. STREET. MORNING.   112

     TRUMAN exchanges a cheery greeting with SPENCER.

                         SPENCER
          How are ya, Truman?

                         TRUMAN
          Inhale...exhale...same old thing.

     He waves to the WASHINGTONS across the street. He pets
     PLUTO the dog.

113 INT. OFFICE. DAY.   113

     Back at work at the insurance company, TRUMAN sits in his
     cubicle making another of his cold calls.

                         TRUMAN
          --a forty-two year old woman sitting in
          the second row at an amateur production
          of Hamlet, Hamlet's dagger slips from his
          hand and flies into the audience...

     A YOUNG WOMAN, carrying a stack of files, catches Truman's eye
     as she passes. VIVIAN. She is faintly reminiscent of Sylvia
     at the same age - even wearing a similar sweater.

                         TRUMAN
                   (returning to his call)
          --what I'm saying is, life is a fragile
          thing...hullo?

114 EXT. TRUMAN'S BACKYARD. DUSK.   114

     TRUMAN wheels his lawnmower, deliberately averting his eyes
     from the back of the house. Staring out of the kitchen
     window, a tall glass of iced tea in her hand, MERYL has been

(CONTINUED)

114   CONTINUED: 114

        anticipating her husband's appearance. She wears a
        neckbrace, we sense more as a reminder to Truman than for any
        medical benefit she might derive.

        Feeling Meryl's eyes burning into his back, Truman fires up
        the mower and heads directly towards the symbolically uncut
        section of grass. We focus on the errant blades of grass as
        they are severed by the mower - a new Elk Rotary. The lawn
        is now uniformly trimmed - Truman's final act of defiance
        laid to rest.

115   INT. STUDIO - CONFERENCE ROOM. NIGHT.   115

        CHRISTOF stands at a large, specially screened window,
        silhouetted against the twinkling stars and full moon of a
        hyper-real nightsky.

        Members of the cast enter the room - principal characters in
        Truman's life - MERYL, MARLON, MOTHER, KIRK, TYRONE, LAWRENCE
        and the new actress, VIVIAN. They take their places around a
        long, oval table for a story conference - Vivian sitting
        slightly apart from the rest of the cast.

        We glimpse over Christof's shoulder at what he sees - the
        town of Seahaven far below, bathed in moonlight. He comes
        out of his reverie and joins his cast, sitting at the head of
        the table. In front of him, a TV "tablet" plays silently -
        showing Truman drinking a glass of milk in his kitchen.

                         CHRISTOF
                   (to the assembled cast)
                First of all, I'd like to welcome Walter
                back onto the show.
                   (nods in Kirk's direction)
                You may have done us more of a favor than
                you ever imagined.
                   (turning to Meryl, using her
                   real name)
                Regrettably, I also have to inform you
                that Hannah has chosen not to renew her
                contract.

        All eyes turn to Meryl. She looks at the floor.

                         CHRISTOF
                I'm sure we can all respect her reasons.

        Meryl receives a sympathetic squeeze of the hand from her co-
        star Marlon, now out of wardrobe, wearing an Armani suit.

                                                          (CONTINUED)

115   CONTINUED: 115

                         CHRISTOF
          As you all know, we have already begun to
          orchestrate her break-up from Truman.
                    (more up-beat)
          However, on a more optimistic note, I'm
          pleased to announce that television's
          first on-air conception will still take
          place. You witnessed the initial contact
          this morning.
                    (glancing to Vivien, once
                    again using her real name)
          You all know Claudia from her work in
          theatre.

                         MOTHER
          I loved your Ophelia.

                         CLAUDIA
          Why thank you.

     The rest of the cast nod politely in Claudia's direction.
     CHLOE passes out a bound document to each cast member.

                         CHRISTOF
                    (referring to the documents)
          This is a copy of Claudia's back story.
          Her character's name is "Vivien".

     The cast idly flips through the documents, prominently
     stamped on the cover, "NOT TO BE TAKEN ON SET".

                         CHRISTOF
          We intend to entice Truman into the affair
          as soon as possible. Claudia will make a
          pass at the insurance seminar Truman's
          attending. Details are in your schedules.
                    (pause for effect)
          I don't have to tell you how critical the
          next few weeks will be. This takes us
          into the next generation. When Truman's
          child is born, the network will be
          switching to a two-channel format to
          chronicle both lives.

                         CLAUDIA
          What happens when Truman and the baby are
          both on camera together?

                         CHRISTOF
          There will simply be duplicate coverage.

115   CONTINUED: (2)   115

                                CLAUDIA
                          (mischievous)
                    Let's just hope we don't have twins.

                                MARLON
                          (uncharacteristically
                          flippant)
                    When Truman dies do we go back to the
                    single channel?

        The cast turns in his direction. Christof shoots him a
        disapproving look.

116   INT. TRUMAN'S BASEMENT. NIGHT.   116

        TRUMAN sleeps on a cot bed in his basement - more cluttered
        than usual. A virtual bombsite - dozens of cardboard boxes
        stacked everywhere. Although he is covered in bedding, his
        sock-clad feet stick out of the bed covers. The outline of
        his body is still clearly visible. He snores quietly.

117   INT. VARIOUS VIEWER LOCATIONS. NIGHT.   117

        The TWO OLD LADIES have nodded off on their sofa in front of
        the television, their breathing and occasional snores echo
        those of Truman.

        In the BAR, the WAITRESS - normally an avid viewer - only idly
        glances to the screen as she passes with a tray of drinks.

        The MAN in the bath resignedly lets the water out of the tub
        and goes to get out.

        The MOTHER only occasionally glances to the screen as she
        feeds her BABY. Her DAUGHTER has her eyes closed, bopping to
        her Walkman.

118   INT. CONTROL ROOM. NIGHT.   118

        SIMEON sits at his control desk, directing the "night-shift".
        He pays scant attention to the big screen, giving his
        instructions in a lethargic, metronomic manner.

                                SIMEON
                    ...Ready two. Go to two.

        An OPERATOR, eating a slice of pizza, presses one of the
        illuminated buttons on the panel and the camera angle changes
        to a close shot of Truman's covered head. The camera stays on
        the blanketed head for a long moment.

                                                        (CONTINUED)

118   CONTINUED: 118

                         SIMEON
              And back to the medium...

Another button is pressed and the angle changed. A trace of
frustration is evident in the control room. Recording a
sleeping subject is unrewarding enough without also having to
contend with Truman's recently acquired camera-shyness.

                         SIMEON
              ...and wide...

                         OPERATOR
                    (aside to Simeon)
              What a loser.

                         SIMEON
              Who cares? Makes life easier for us.
              He is what he is.

At the far end of the control room, one of the large double doors
opens and CHRISTOF enters, dressed in a smoking jacket. Simeon and
the Operators subtly straighten in their chairs. Christof pretends
not to notice. He is staring intently at the ON-AIR monitor.

                         CHRISTOF
              Why is he in the basement?

                         SIMEON
              He moved down there after Meryl packed up
              and left.

                         CHRISTOF
              Why wasn't I told? Any unpredictable
              behavior has to be reported.
                    (returning to the screen)
              Is that the best shot we can get?

                         SIMEON
              What's to see?

                         CHRISTOF
              What's on the ClockCam?

The operator punches up the camera hidden inside a broken
cuckoo clock. A box obscures the view.

                         OPERATOR
              There's an obstruction.

Christof watches Truman, a trace of concern in his eyes.
CHLOE enters.

                                                    (CONTINUED)

> CHRISTOF
> (referring to the debris in
> Truman's basement)
> What happened down there?

> SIMEON
> He was tidying up his garbage.
> (sensing Christof's concern)
> I was going to call you. But half-way
> through, he gave up and fell asleep.

Apparently satisfied, Christof turns to an Operator.

> CHRISTOF
> I want to check the set-ups for
> tomorrow's insurance convention.

Reading off the notes in Chloe's folder, the Operator punches up
a batch of camera angles on smaller preview monitors. They show
a generic-looking hotel, devoid of actors. A banner in reception
reads, *"Welcome Seahaven Life and Accident"*.

The Operator looks to Christof for approval and realizes his
producer's attention has wandered. Christof has wandered
down to the front of the room to stand beside the giant ON-
AIR monitor still displaying the sleeping figure of Truman.

> CHRISTOF
> Give me a shot from Truman's ring.

> SIMEON
> He gave it back to his father.

Christof nods.

> CHRISTOF
> (a trace of concern)
> Why is he so still?

Christof picks up a spare headset from the panel and puts it
to his ear.

> CHRISTOF
> Isolate the audio.

An operator pushes up an audio fader on the panel. Christof
and his colleagues listen to Truman's steady breathing in
their headphones.

> SIMEON
> (shrugs)
> He's still breathing.

118   CONTINUED: (3)   118

        Simeon and the Operators nod, reassured that nothing is
        amiss. Christof is not so easily convinced.

                            CHRISTOF
                Give me a preview. An ECU on his torso.

        A camera hidden in the room's lamp zooms in to Truman's prone
        outline. While the breathing remains steady, the body does
        not rise and fall. Christof, still listening to his
        headphones, detects a faint scratching sound followed by a
        strange thud.

                            CHRISTOF
                    (anxious, barking a command
                    to Chloe)
                Phone him.

        Chloe picks up a phone connected to the desk and dials.

                            CHRISTOF
                    (anticipating Chloe's
                    question)
                Tell him it's a wrong number.

        The upstairs phone begins to ring. Truman doesn't flinch.

119   INT.   AN OFFICE BUILDING SOMEWHERE - RECEPTION.   NIGHT.   119

        The TWO SECURITY GUARDS are intrigued by Truman's unanswered
        phone on their television set.

120   INT.   CONTROL ROOM. NIGHT.   120

        CHRISTOF and SIMEON concentrate on another, separate monitor
        playing in fast-rewind, time code in the bottom right-hand
        corner. It is a recording of the night's transmission.
        Simeon pauses on the last on-camera appearance by Truman.

        They watch Truman, on-screen, switch off the basement light
        and climb into the cot bed fully clothed, immediately pulling
        the covers over his head. As the light is switched off, the
        recording camera automatically switches to night vision.
        Simeon continues to play at normal speed, now and then
        scrolling forward in fast-forward mode. Christof suddenly
        points to the screen.

                            CHRISTOF
                There. Freeze...Zoom into the chair...

        Simeon types the appropriate command.

                                                            (CONTINUED)

120   CONTINUED: 120

                          CHRISTOF
                 Enhance...there!

On the blown-up screen, between a cardboard box and a chair
leg, it is barely possible to make out Truman's hand as he
crawls commando-style from beneath the covers and behind a
cardboard box near the large tool cupboard.

Simeon points out an angle of the empty staircase.

                          SIMEON
                 He hasn't gone up the stairs. He's still
                 in the room.

121   EXT. TRUMAN'S HOUSE. NIGHT.   121

MARLON's car squeals to a halt outside Truman's house.
Hurriedly dressed in jeans and coat over a bare chest, he
dashes barefoot up the porch to the front door. He tries the
doorhandle, pounds on the door and rings the doorbell
simultaneously, shouting Truman's name all the while.

                          MARLON
                 Tru!..Tru!...Earthquake alert...flood!
                 We've gotta get outside onto the
                 street! Tru?!

Frustrated, Marlon picks up one of Meryl's carefully nurtured
flower pots from beneath the porch window.

                          MARLON
                      (shouting a warning)
                 I'm coming in, Tru!

Marlon hurls the flower pot through the window.

122   INT. TRUMAN'S HOUSE - BASEMENT. NIGHT.   122

MARLON switches on the light and clambers down the wooden
stairs to the basement.

He pushes away the clutter and finally stands at his co-star's
bedside. He gingerly lifts the covers. Beneath the bedding,
clothes have been carefully piled to resemble a sleeping
figure - socks placed on the end of two tree branches.

Buried amongst the clothes is Truman's portable tape recorder.
Marlon places the recorder next to his ear. The cassette plays
the sound of TRUMAN BREATHING.

123   INT.   CONTROL ROOM.   NIGHT.   123

CHRISTOF stares, wide-eyed, at the image on the On-Air
monitor of MARLON.

                    CHRISTOF
            Find him, Marlon!

124   INT.   BASEMENT.   NIGHT.   124

MARLON starts frantically pushing aside the clutter, sending
Truman's model ships and other hobbies crashing to the floor.
Eliminating all other possible hiding places, he confronts
Truman's tool closet, the wall map of the Fiji Islands still
hanging on the door. Marlon rips open the door and is hit
with a shaft of light - moonlight.

The top of the closet has been removed and a crude tunnel
containing a ladder heads almost directly upwards to the
outside of the house. The bottom of the closet is ankle deep
with dirt. Embedded in the tunnel wall is Meryl's Chef's
Mate - Truman's digging implement.

124A   EXT.   TRUMAN'S HOUSE.   NIGHT.   124A

MARLON's head pops up outside the house. Unable to help
himself, Marlon looks directly into a wide shot camera
concealed in a streetlight.

125   INT.   CONTROL ROOM.   NIGHT.   125

                    CHRISTOF
            Marlon, don't look at the camera!
            Say something!

                    MARLON
                (to streetlight, stunned,
                breaking the fourth wall)
            What? He's gone!

                    CHRISTOF
                (to Simeon, quiet but firm)
            Cut transmission.

Simeon hesitates, unsure if he has heard correctly. He looks
to Christof for confirmation, his finger poised over an
"EMERGENCY" button.

                                                        (CONTINUED)

125   CONTINUED: 125

                              CHRISTOF
                            (enraged)
                    I said, "Cut!"

        Christof lunges forward and presses the button himself. The
        scene in Truman's bedroom playing on the on-air monitor is
        abruptly replaced by the "TRUMAN" logo and the message,
        "TECHNICAL FAULT. PLEASE STAND BY."

126   INT. A LIVING ROOM SOMEWHERE. NIGHT.   126

        The TWO OLD WOMEN on the sofa are stunned to see their TV
        screen go blank.

127   INT. A BAR SOMEWHERE. NIGHT.   127

        HEADS also turn in the bar permanently tuned to the "Truman"
        channel.

128   INT. AN APARTMENT SOMEWHERE. NIGHT.   128

        The other loyal viewer transfixed by the test card is SYLVIA,
        alone in her darkened apartment.

129   INT. CONTROL ROOM. NIGHT.   129

        Reminiscent of a military headquarters in wartime, the
        control room is a scene of barely controlled panic. SECURITY
        GUARDS come and go, phones ring, lights flash, every
        available VIDEO MIXER is working. The monitors - the "eyes"
        of the searchers - are systematically scrutinized for any
        sign of Truman. CHRISTOF orchestrates operations from his
        position at the center of the control panel.

                              SIMEON
                            (nervous)
                    We've declared a curfew. Everyone else
                    is at first positions.

                              CHRISTOF
                    All prop cars accounted for?

                              SIMEON
                    He has to be on foot. He has the
                    world's most recognizable face. He
                    can't disappear.

130   EXT. SEAHAVEN - MAIN STREET. NIGHT.   130

     We pan down one empty street after another. The town center is
     totally, eerily deserted. Suddenly, a line of PEOPLE comes
     around the corner, fanned out across the street - a man-hunt.

     PEOPLE of every description, shoulder to shoulder, marching
     down the otherwise empty streets the way a search is
     conducted at a crime scene. The lines include PRINCIPALS and
     EXTRAS linked arm in arm, wardrobed for their usual roles as
     EXECUTIVES and SECRETARIES, STORE CLERKS, TELEPHONISTS,
     MAINTENANCE and CONSTRUCTION WORKERS, WAITERS and WAITRESSES,
     COOKS, SHOPPERS, HEALTH WORKERS, SECURITY GUARDS, POSTAL
     WORKERS, POLICE OFFICERS, FIRE FIGHTERS and HOMELESS PEOPLE.

     We occasionally glimpse Truman's friends and colleagues
     amongst the searchers - MARLON, LAWRENCE, MOTHER & KIRK,
     VIVIEN and TYRONE. Even the WASHINGTON's and SPENCER and
     PLUTO have joined the search - a snarling Pluto straining at
     the leash has now assumed the role of tracker dog - Truman's
     pajamas waved in front of his nose (clearly miscast as the
     friendly, neighborhood pooch).

     Searchlights from Seahaven's many towers sweep the town.
     Once, the light falls on a blackened face cowering in the
     bushes beside a picket fence - the fence now faintly
     reminiscent of prison bars. Even the beam of the full moon
     appears to be sweeping the town like a searchlight.

131   EXT. BRIDGE. NIGHT.   131

     Barriers have been erected at the bridge leading out of
     Seahaven, guarded by several Seahaven police cars.

     An extra dressed as a DERELICT wheels his shopping cart
     towards the bridge.

     The derelict takes a look along the walkway alongside the
     bridge as if participating in the search. He finds a POLICE
     OFFICER standing on the walkway.

                         POLICEMAN OFFICER
               Any sign of him?

                         DERELICT
                    (gravelly voice)
               Not yet.

                         POLICE OFFICER
               Take it easy.

131A   INT.   CONTROL ROOM.   NIGHT.   131A

A VIDEO OPERATOR in the sixth row watches the scene on one of
his monitors - the derelict standing with his back to camera.
Just as the derelict turns towards camera the Operator turns
away to take a sip of coffee. He misses what we see on his
monitor - the derelict's blackened face belongs to TRUMAN.

131B   EXT.   BRIDGE.   NIGHT.   131B

The disguised TRUMAN heads back to town.

132   INT.   CONTROL ROOM.   NIGHT.   132

CHRISTOF turns to a LIGHTING TECHNICIAN.

                    CHRISTOF
          We need more light.

133   EXT.   SEAHAVEN STREETS.   NIGHT.   133

A building-to-building, floor-to-floor, office-to-office
search is also being conducted, each structure secured as
they go - the SEARCHERS Paying special attention to potential
blind spots such as closets, dumpsters, man holes, sewers,
car trunks, trees and shrubbery.

We focus on one of the waves of searchers. TRUMAN has linked
arms in the middle of a row, his disguise still holding up.

134   INT.   CONTROL ROOM.   NIGHT.   134

CHRISTOF glances impatiently at his watch.

                    CHRISTOF
          We'll never find him like this. What
          time is it?

                    CHLOE
               (anticipating the request)
          It's too early.

                    CHRISTOF
          It doesn't matter. Cue the sun.

135   EXT.   STREETS.   NIGHT/DAY.   135

The sun instantly rises over Seahaven. CAST and EXTRAS shade
their eyes from the sudden glare.

136   INT.   CONTROL ROOM.   NIGHT.   136

While his COLLEAGUES monitor the bank of screens, CHRISTOF
has been joined by the two anxious studio executives, MOSES
and ROMAN.

                    MOSES
               (to Christof who is still
               studying the faces in a row of
               SEARCHERS)
          Rumors are circulating he's dead. The
          media is in a feeding frenzy. The phone
          lines are jammed. Every network has a
          pirated shot of Marlon in the closet.

                    ROMAN
               (pacing nervously)
          The sponsors are threatening to rip up
          their contracts.

                    CHRISTOF
               (unconcerned, referring to the
               static "STAND BY" graphic, now
               accompanied by soothing
               classical music)
          Why? We're getting higher ratings for
          that graphic than any time in the show's
          history.

137   INT.   BAR.   NIGHT.   137

The television above the bar carries the test card.   PATRONS
animatedly discuss Truman's fate over their drinks.   Some
place bets with each other on Truman's fate.

138   EXT.   ELECTRONICS STORE.   NIGHT.   138

A CROWD of passersby hover around a display of televisions in
the window of an electronics store, awaiting developments.

139   INT.   CONTROL ROOM.   NIGHT.   139

The fan of EXTRAS reaches the harbor and automatically turns
to make another sweep.

                                              (CONTINUED)

139   CONTINUED: 139

                              CHLOE
                    (referring to the empty streets)
               When we flush him out how do we
               explain this?

                              CHRISTOF
                    (deadpan)
               We tell him the truth.

          CHLOE looks askance at CHRISTOF.

                              CHRISTOF
                    (joking darkly)
               We're making a movie.

140   EXT. HARBORSIDE. DAY.   140

          TRUMAN has broken away from the line of SEARCHERS.

          However, as he bypasses the entrance to a ticket box, he
          hasn't bargained on coming face to face with another
          straggler from the search.

          MARLON. Truman freezes in front of his childhood companion -
          Marlon instantly seeing through Truman's homeless disguise.

          Truman glances nervously in the direction of the searchers.
          Their backs to the two men, they are beginning their next
          sweep. One shout from Marlon will give Truman away - he is
          at Marlon's mercy.

          Without a word, Marlon walks past Truman and rejoins the search.

          Truman glances back to Marlon's retreating figure but Marlon
          never looks back.

141   EXT. DOCKSIDE. DAY.   141

          TRUMAN reaches the edge of the dock. He looks out over the
          bay. There, riding at anchor some two hundred yards out, is
          a sail boat - the same boat that circled Kirk and Truman's
          sail boat many years earlier.

          We see a close up of Truman's terrified eyes in his blackened
          face, staring down at the lapping water. He steels himself,
          shuts out the doubts and dives into the water.

142   INT.   CONTROL ROOM.   NIGHT.   142

                         SIMEON
                      (hopeful)
             I'm sure we'll get him on this next sweep.

                         CHRISTOF
                      (distracted)
             What have we missed?

                         SIMEON
             It's just a matter of time.

CHRISTOF concentrates on a monitor displaying a view of
the harbor.

                         CHRISTOF
                      (to Simeon)
             We're not watching the sea.

                         SIMEON
                      (confused)
             Why would we--

                         CHRISTOF
             Sweep the harbor.

His COLLEAGUES begin to flick through dozens of waterborne
hidden camera shots - in moored craft, lighthouses and buoys
- trying to locate Truman.

Suddenly on one of the monitors there appears a single sail
etched against the horizon.

                         SIMEON
             That's got to be him!

                         ROMAN
             How can he sail?! He's in insurance!

                         CHRISTOF
             Resume transmission.

Simeon punches a button and the image of the sail boat is
instantly transferred to the large ON-AIR Monitor.

143   INT.   OLD WOMEN'S APARTMENT.   NIGHT.   143

The TWO OLD WOMEN doze against each other on the sofa in
front of the TV.

                                                    (CONTINUED)

143 CONTINUED: 143

The classical music on the television is abruptly replaced by
the sound of the wind and the sea. One Old Lady blinks her
eyes open, her breath taken away by the sight of Truman at
the wheel of the sail boat. She rouses her companion.

144 INT. CONTROL ROOM. NIGHT.   144

                    CHRISTOF
              (staring intently at the
              ON-AIR monitor)
         What do we have on that boat?

SIMEON scans a computer shot list. He types in a code.

A camera from the mast of Truman's sail boat activates. Truman,
unaware of the camera, is concentrating on his sailing.

145 EXT. HARBOR. DAY.   145

By now the ocean spray has washed most of the dirt from
TRUMAN's face - only a residue remains. The rags he wears
are soaked.

As he steers, he occasionally refers to a *HOW TO SAIL* book
from his coat pocket.

146 INT. A BATHROOM SOMEWHERE. NIGHT.   146

The MAN in the bath we have seen earlier continues to watch
from his tub.

                    MAN
              (to himself)
         I knew he wasn't dead.

147 EXT. HARBOR. DAY.   147

TRUMAN is at the wheel of the sail boat, wind filling her sails.

Seahaven left far behind, his is the only craft afloat in the
harbor. He sets a course for the open sea as he and his
father did long ago.

148 INT. CONTROL ROOM. NIGHT.   148

CHRISTOF and the other PRODUCTION STAFF watch TRUMAN from a
buoy's POV as he sails by.

                                              (CONTINUED)

148   CONTINUED: 148

                              CHRISTOF
                    Get another boat.

                              CHLOE
                    The ferry.

148A   EXT. FERRY TERMINAL. DAY.   148A

       A PRODUCTION ASSISTANT runs down the dock towards the FERRY
       CAPTAIN and his CREW.

                         PRODUCTION ASSISTANT
                    Get that boat out there!

                              FERRY CAPTAIN
                         (who also played the bus driver)
                    I don't know how. We were just told to
                    put on these clothes.

149   EXT. HARBOR. DAY.   149

       The sea choppier now, rising and falling steeply beneath his
       boat, TRUMAN nears a large buoy bobbing clumsily in the
       strong swell. An official-looking sign on the buoy reads -
       "DANGEROUS WATERS. DO NOT ENTER." We see an extreme close
       up of the nautical signpost where a disguised miniature
       camera tracks Truman's progress.

150   INT. CONTROL ROOM. NIGHT.   150

                              ROMAN
                         (anxious)
                    How do we stop him?

                              CHRISTOF
                         (glancing to Simeon)
                    How else?

       Christof nods to controls on the mixing desk marked, "WIND"
       and "RAIN".

151   EXT. HARBOR. DAY.   151

       Storm clouds roll towards TRUMAN's boat at an alarming speed.
       He looks back towards the Seahaven skyline, rapidly receding
       behind him. Doubts invade Truman's head but he shuts them
       out and steers into the teeth of the storm - a look of
       resolve in his eyes we have never witnessed before.

152   INT. CONTROL ROOM. NIGHT.   152

        MOSES and ROMAN pace at the back of the control room.
        CHRISTOF is focused on his monitor. Like Truman, he steels
        himself for a fight.

                         CHRISTOF
                 Cue music...

                         SIMEON
                    (hesitant)
                 What music?

                         CHRISTOF
                    (irritated)
                 Storm music...Wagner...

                         CHLOE
                    (watching the monitor)
                 There's no rescue boat in the area. He
                 won't know what to do.

                         MOSES
                    (trying to appeal to
                    Christof's sense of reason)
                 For God's sake, Chris. The whole world
                 is watching. We can't let him die in
                 front of a live audience.

                         CHRISTOF
                 He was born in front of a live audience.
                    (never taking his eyes from
                    the screen)
                 Don't worry, he's not willing to risk his
                 life. His doubts will turn him back.

        Simeon reluctantly winds the controls for *"WAVE"*, *"WIND"* and
        "RAIN" towards their maximum settings.

                         CHRISTOF
                 Kill the lights.

153   EXT. HARBOR. DAY.   153

        Darkness suddenly descends. High winds and horizontal
        driving rain buffet the boat. TRUMAN fights the tiller.
        Hurricane force winds shake the mast and keel, ripping the
        sails to shreds.

        Suddenly, the mast of Truman's boat is struck by a bolt of
        lightning - snapping the rigging and knocking Truman
        overboard. Flailing in the tempest, Truman manages to grab

(CONTINUED)

153   CONTINUED: 153

hold of a trailing rope from the mast and hand-over-hand
drags himself back on board. Truman takes the rope and
lashes himself to the wheel.

Monstrous waves continually submerge the boat. With what
little is left of his rigging, Truman continues to head into
the gale.

                    TRUMAN
               (shouting above the storm,
               screaming up to the sky)
          Come on, is that the best you can do?
          You're gonna have to kill me!

154   INT. CONTROL ROOM. NIGHT.   154

In contrast to his panic-striken COLLEAGUES, CHRISTOF gives
an outward appearance of calm. Only we witness the minute
bead of sweat appearing at his temple that betrays him.

                    SIMEON
               (shocked at the sight of Truman
               binding himself to the boat)
          Is he out of his mind?

                    MOSES
               (to Christof)
          On behalf of the studio, I demand that
          you cease transmission.

                    CHRISTOF
               (defiant, to Operators)
          Keep running!

                    MOSES
          --That's not for you to say.

                    CHRISTOF
          I take full responsibility--

                    MOSES
          --I'm telling you for the last time.

                    CHRISTOF
               (to OPERATOR in front of
               radar-style screen)
          How close is he?

                    OPERATOR
          Very close.

                                              (CONTINUED)

154   CONTINUED: 154

                          CHRISTOF
                 Capsize him! Tip him over!

                          MOSES
                      (overlapping)
                 For God's sake, Christof!

                          CHLOE
                      (unable to contain herself
                      any longer, entreating
                      Christof)
                 You can't! He's tied himself to the
                 boat. He'll drown!

                          SIMEON
                      (staring at Truman on the
                      monitor, becoming affected by
                      his display of courage)
                 He doesn't care.

                          CHRISTOF
                      (enraged, to the Operators)
                 Do it!

All eyes turn in Christof's direction. None of the Operators
is willing to touch the controls.

Christof reaches to the panel and does it himself, turning
the *"WAVE"* controls to their maximum settings.

154A   EXT. OCEAN. DAY.   154A

A series of giant breakers march in formation across the sea
- arising from an unseen source.

155   EXT. OCEAN. DAY.   155

The waves break across Truman's vessel. TRUMAN appears to be
losing his fight against the storm, each successive wave
taking its toll on his body, sapping his strength, his
bindings the only thing keeping him upright. His head
slumps, the tiller goes loose in his grasp, rocking out of
control. Truman's will is draining away.

156   INT. CONTROL ROOM. NIGHT.   156

The control room CREW watch the heroic image of Truman on the
ON-AIR monitor, awestruck, as if they too are now spectators
watching a movie.

157   EXT. OCEAN. DAY.   157

As he is about to be overcome by the next wave, TRUMAN
clamps the wheel with his whole body and braces for one
last wave.

But the wave does not come. A strange phenomenon is
occurring in the ocean. A distinct division has appeared in
the ocean swell. Between the large rolling waves lies a
corridor of calmer water, several hundred yards wide, a
curious escape lane. The wind and the rain are also
subsiding, the darkness lifting. A mist clings to the
surface of the water. Truman steers his sail boat down the
eerie corridor.

Several large, dark shapes emerge on the horizon. Land?
Islands? The shapes, containing some enormous mechanism
including a huge wheel, only half exposed above water level,
appear to be the source of the peculiar wave formations.

Truman continues to steer his wrecked sailboat towards the
infinitely receding horizon. All is calm until we see the
bow of the boat suddenly strike a huge, blue wall, knocking
Truman off his feet. Truman recovers and clambers across the
deck to the bow of the boat. Looming above him out of the
sea is a cyclorama of colossal dimensions. The sky he has
been sailing towards is nothing but a painted backdrop.
Truman looks upward, straining his eyes to see the top of the
sky, but it curves away at a steep angle beyond his sight.

Clinging to the boat with one hand, he tentatively reaches
out towards the painted cyclorama. He touches the sky.

He looks about him and simply laughs.

158   INT. CONTROL ROOM. NIGHT.   158

CHRISTOF and his PRODUCTION STAFF take in Truman's reaction
in stunned silence.

159   INT/EXT.   BARROOM/LAUNDROMAT/STOREFRONT/APARTMENT. NIGHT.   159

Truman's laugh echoes around bars, offices, shops, homes and
streets - wherever a television is to be found - no VIEWER
speaks. They too are stunned into a hushed expectancy. The
collective audience holds its breath.

160   EXT. OCEAN/CYCLORAMA. DAY.   160

As the boat drifts alongside the seemingly never-ending curve
of the cyclorama, TRUMAN's attention is drawn to an outline
in the otherwise flawless backdrop. He retrieves the
identikit picture of Sylvia from his coat pocket and clambers
to the prow of the boat.

There, camouflaged in the painted skyscape just above the
water line, is a door. Truman grabs hold of the recessed
doorhandle and halts the drifting boat. He stands in front
of the door and closes his eyes in a silent prayer.

161   INT. CONTROL ROOM. NIGHT.   161

The control room CREW stare in silence at the monitor - their
very livelihood on the brink of vanishing. CHRISTOF opens a
small panel on his desk, breaks a seal, and speaks into the
emergency P.A. system that is linked to the entire studio.

                    CHRISTOF
              Truman!

162   INT/EXT. OCEAN/CYCLORAMA. DAY.   162

CHRISTOF's voice booms over the now calm ocean.

                    CHRISTOF
              Truman!

TRUMAN drops the handle as if his hand has been burned. He
looks all about him.

                    CHRISTOF (O.C.)
              You can speak. I can hear you.

Truman takes a moment to overcome his fear and astonishment.

                       TRUMAN
                 Who are you?

                       CHRISTOF
                 I'm the creator.

Truman looks up to the "heavens".

                       TRUMAN
                 The creator of what?

                                        (CONTINUED)

162 CONTINUED: 162

                       CHRISTOF (O.C.)
        A show - that gives hope and joy and
        inspiration to millions.

                       TRUMAN
          (incredulous)
        A show. Then who am I?

                       CHRISTOF (O.C.)
        You're the star.

Truman struggles to take it all in.

                       TRUMAN
        Nothing was real.

                       CHRISTOF
        You were real. That's what made you
        so good to watch.

Truman takes out the drenched picture of Sylvia, recalling
her words at the beach.

                       TRUMAN
          (to himself)
        "The eyes are everywhere."

163 INT. CONTROL ROOM. NIGHT.   163

CHRISTOF picks up a slim, flat monitor. He swivels in his
chair and gazes intently at the image of Truman he now holds in
his hands.

                       CHRISTOF
        Listen to me, Truman--

On the screen, Truman again reaches for the door handle.

164 EXT. CYCLORAMA. DAY.   164

We focus on TRUMAN's hand. CHRISTOF's voice echoes across
the water.

                       CHRISTOF
        You can leave if you want. I won't try
        to stop you. But you won't survive out
        there. You don't know what to do,
        where to go.

A wave of doubt washes over Truman's face.

                             (CONTINUED)

164   CONTINUED: 164

                    TRUMAN
                (referring to the photo)
          I have a map.

                    CHRISTOF
          Truman, I've watched you your whole life.
          I saw you take your first step, your
          first word, your first kiss. I know you
          better than you know yourself. You're
          not going to walk out that door--

                    TRUMAN
          --You never had a camera in my head.

165   INT/EXT. VARIOUS LOCATIONS. NIGHT.   165

      The VIEWERS stare into camera in fascination.

166   INT. CONTROL ROOM. NIGHT.   166

      TRUMAN turns back to the sky, looking up towards CHRISTOF.

                    CHRISTOF
          Truman, there's no more truth out
          there than in the world I created for
          you - the same lies and deceit. But
          in my world you have nothing to fear.

      Truman seems to be considering the possibilities. He looks
      to the identikit picture of Sylvia in his hand.

                    CHRISTOF
                (suddenly angry)
          Say something, damn it! You're still on
          camera, live to the world...!

167   INT. A ROOM SOMEWHERE. NIGHT.   167

      SYLVIA gazes at the picture of herself on her television
      screen as if it is her reflection in the mirror.

168   EXT. CYCLORAMA. DAY.   168

      TRUMAN opens the door in the sky.

      He hesitates. Perhaps he cannot go through with it after
      all. The camera slowly zooms into Truman's face.

                                                        (CONTINUED)

168   CONTINUED: 168

                              TRUMAN
                  In case I don't see you--good afternoon,
                  good evening and good night.

He steps through the door and is gone. Silence. Then -

169   INT/EXT. VIEWERS. NIGHT.   169

Spontaneous jubilation from VIEWERS in their various locations
- bars, homes and offices. We follow the figure of SYLVIA,
running through the streets. Some of the viewers outside an
electronics store glimpse her as she runs by.

170   INT. CONTROL ROOM. NIGHT.   170

Even the cynical SIMEON jumps out of his seat - for the first
time in the film - and lets out a joyous whoop, forgetting
himself for a moment, caught up in the drama.

                              SIMEON
                  Yes!

Self-conscious, he takes his seat again almost immediately.
His COLLEAGUES are transfixed by the live ON-AIR monitor
continuing to play its only available shot, the open door in
the sky.

Gradually, the attention of those in the control room shifts
from the monitor to CHRISTOF. He sits slumped, staring at
the open door in the sky.

Eventually MOSES looks to Simeon. Moses nods to the "ON AIR"
button. Simeon presses the button and the screen - the movie
screen - goes to static.

171   MONTAGE/END TITLES.   171

Highlights from *Truman - Total Record of a Human Life* begin
to play.

                                                 FADE OUT

CAST AND CREW CREDITS

PARAMOUNT PICTURES PRESENTS
A SCOTT RUDIN PRODUCTION
A PETER WEIR FILM

JIM CARREY

THE TRUMAN SHOW

LAURA LINNEY   NOAH EMMERICH

NATASCHA MCELHONE

HOLLAND TAYLOR   BRIAN DELATE

UNA DAMON   PAUL GIAMATTI   PHILIP BAKER HALL

PETER KRAUSE   JOHN PLESHETTE   HEIDI SCHANZ

HARRY SHEARER   BLAIR SLATER

and ED HARRIS

Directed by	Edited by	Casting by
PETER WEIR	WILLIAM ANDERSON, A.C.E.	HOWARD FEUER
Written by	LEE SMITH	Unit Production Managers
ANDREW NICCOL	Original Music by	RICHARD LUKE ROTHSCHILD
Produced by	BURKHARD DALLWITZ	JOSEPH P. KANE
SCOTT RUDIN ANDREW NICCOL	Costume Designer	First Assistant Director
Produced by	MARILYN MATTHEWS	ALAN B. CURTISS
EDWARD S. FELDMAN ADAM SCHROEDER	Special Design Consultant	Second Assistant Director
Director of Photography	WENDY STITES	JONATHAN WATSON
PETER BIZIOU, B.S.C.	Executive Producer	Visual Effects Supervisor
Production Designer	LYNN PLESHETTE	MICHEAL J. McALISTER
DENNIS GASSNER	Co-Producer	
	RICHARD LUKE ROTHSCHILD	

CAST

Player	Role	Player	Role

TRUMAN'S WORLD

Truman Burbank . . . . JIM CARREY
Meryl . . . . LAURA LINNEY
Marlon . . . . NOAH EMMERICH
Lauren/Sylvia . . . . NATASCHA McELHONE
Truman's Mother . . . . HOLLAND TAYLOR
Truman's Father . . . . BRIAN DELATE
Young Truman . . . . BLAIR SLATER
Lawrence . . . . PETER KRAUSE
Vivien . . . . HEIDI SCHANZ
Ron and Don . . . . RON TAYLOR
                                            DON TAYLOR
Spencer . . . . TED RAYMOND
Travel Agent . . . . JUDY CLAYTON
Truman's Neighbors . . . . . . FRITZ DOMINIQUE
                                       ANGEL SCHMIEDT
                                    NASTASSJA SCHMIEDT
Teacher . . . . MURIEL MOORE
News Vendor . . . . MAL JONES
Insurance Co-Worker . . . . . . JUDSON VAUGHN
Ferry Worker . . . . EARL HILLIARD, JR.
Bus Driver/Ferry Captain DAVID ANDREW NASH
Bus Supervisor . . . . JIM TOWERS
Little Girl in Bus . . . . SAVANNAH SWAFFORD
Security Guards . . . . ANTONI CORONE
                              MARIO ERNESTO SANCHEZ
Man at Beach . . . . JOHN ROSELIUS
Truman (4 years) . . . . KADE COATES
Nurse . . . . MARCIA DeBONIS
Surgeon . . . . SAM KITCHIN
Orderly . . . . SEBASTIAN YOUNGBLOOD
Hospital Security Guard . . . . DAVE COREY
Policeman at Power Plant MARK ALAN GILLOTT
Policemen at Truman's House . . . . JAY SAITER
                                            TONY TODD
Man in Christmas Box . . . . MARCO RUBEO
Couple at Picnic Table . . . . DARYL DAVIS
                                        ROBERT DAVIS
Production Assistant . . . . R.J. MURDOCK
Men at Newstand . . MATTHEW McDONOUGH
                                     LARRY McDOWELL
Ticket Taker . . . . JOSEPH LUCUS

CHRISTOF'S WORLD

Christof . . . . ED HARRIS
Control Room Directors . . . . . . PAUL GIAMATTI
                                         ADAM TOMEI

Mike Michaelson . . . . HARRY SHEARER
Chloe . . . . UNA DAMON
Network Executives . . . . . PHILIP BAKER HALL
                                      JOHN PLESHETTE
Keyboard Artists   PHILIP GLASS
                                        JOHN PRAMIK

THE VIEWERS

Bar Waitresses . . . . O-LAN JONES
                              KRISTA LYNN LANDOLFI
Bartender . . . . JOE MINJARES
Bar Patrons . . . . AL FOSTER
                                        ZOAUNNE LeROY
                                        MILLIE SLAVIN
Man in Bathtub . . . . TERRY CAMILLERI
Senior Citizens . . . . DONA HARDY
                                       JEANETTE MILLER
Garage Attendants . . JOEL McKINNON MILLER
                                         TOM SIMMONS
Mother . . . . SUSAN ANGELO
Daughter . . . . CARLY SMIGA
Japanese Family . . . . YUJI OKUMOTO
                                    KIYOKO YAMAGUCHI
                                     SAEMI NAKAMURA

Stunt Coordinator . . . . PAT BANTA

STUNTS

REESE BANTA	MARTIN GRACE
ANN BELLINGER	AL JONES
JAKE BRAKE	BYRON LEE NASHOLD, JR.
CHARLIE BREWER	LARRY NICHOLAS
MICHAEL CHRISTOPHER	PEEWEE PIEMONTE
SHANE DIXON	STEVE SANTOSUSSO
TIM GILBERT	JIMMY WAITMAN
SANDRA GIMPEL	JOHN ZIMMERMAN

Additional Original Music by . . . . . PHILIP GLASS
Production Supervisor . . . . PHILIP STEUER
Art Director . . . . RICHARD L. JOHNSON
Set Decorator . . . . NANCY HAIGH
Assistant Set Decorator . . . . . PAIGE AUGUSTINE
Assistant Art Director . . . . MARCO RUBEO
Set Designers . . . . THOMAS MINTON
                                  ODIN R. OLDENBURG
Camera Operator . . . . DON REDDY
First Assistant Photographer . . . .
                              WILLIAM M. McCONNELL

110

Second Assistant Photographer . . . .
BILL McCONNELL, JR
B Camera Operators . . . . . . DAVID JOHN GOLIA
ROBERT La BONGE
B Assistant Photographers . . . . BILL COE
TIM BARRY
Second Unit Assistant Photographer . . . . . .
MARK GUTTERUD
Camera Loaders . . . . SUZANNE TRUCKS
JACQUELINE NIVENS
Stills Photographer . . . MELINDA SUE GORDON
Script Supervisor . . . .
WILMA GARSCADDEN-GAHRET
Property Master . . . . . DOUGLAS HARLOCKER
Assistant Property Master . . SCOTT GETZINGER
Second Second Assistant Director . . . .
DAVID BERNSTEIN
Production Sound . . . . ART ROCHESTER
Boom Operators . . . . LINDA MURPHY
RANDY JOHNSON
Cable Person . . . . MARK GRECH
Chief Lighting Technician . . . . KEVIN MURPHY
Assistant Chief Lighting Technicians . . PETER WALTS
PATRIC ABARAVICH
First Company Grip . . . .
CHRISTOPHER CENTRELLA
Dolly Grip . . . . DEAN KING
Second Company Grip . . . . . HUGH McCALLUM
Supervising Make-Up Artists . . . RON BERKELEY
BRAD WILDER
Additional Make-Up Artists . . . .
KATHLEEN BERKELEY
STEPHANIE EASTBURN
Supervising Hairstylists . . . . . . BETTE IVERSON
HAZEL CATMULL
Additional Hairstylists . . . . RONALD SCOTT
ELIZABETH F. LaVALLEE
RANDA SQUILLACOTE
Mr. Carrey's Make-Up Artist . . . . . SHERYL PTAK
Mr. Carrey's Hairstylist . . . . ANNE MORGAN
Costume Supervisor . . . . MARY C. LANE
Set Costumer . CHERYL BEASLEY BLACKWELL
Mr. Carrey's Costumer . . . . ROBERT MATA
Costumers . . . . FRAN ALLGOOD
LINDA PIERCE
Assistant to Mr. Feldman . . . SUSANA R. ZEPEDA
Assistants to Mr. Rudin . . . . MARK ROYBAL
IAN McGLOIN
EDWARD GOEMANS
DANIEL CARB
Assistant to Mr. Weir . . . . . . NOAH ACKERMAN

Assistant to Mr. Niccol . . . . . BRADLEY CRAMP
Assistant to Mr. Carrey . . . . LINDA FIELDS
Second Unit Director . . MICHEAL J. McALISTER
Underwater Camera Operator . . . MIKE THOMAS
Underwater Camera Assistant . . MARYAN ZUREK
Storyboard Illustrator . . . . JOE GRIFFITH
Graphic Designer . . . . ERIC ROSENBERG
Lead Person . . . . MARK WEISSENFLUH
Set Dressers . . . . . . LESLIE "TINKER" LINVILLE
JAMES P. MEEHAN
Assistant Set Dressers . . . RICHARD ANDERSON
DAN SCHULZ
BRIAN SHUPPER
Assistant Property Persons MELANIE S. CHRETIN
GUILLAUME DELOUCHE
Location Managers . ANDREW ULLMAN (Florida)
CHRISTOPHER TROTT (L.A.)
Assistant Location Managers . . . .
BRIANA BURKE (Florida)
JENNIFER DUNNE (L.A.)
Art Department Coordinator . . GAIL LASKOWSKI
Construction Coordinator . . . .
JEFFREY J. PASSANANTE
Construction Foreperson . . . . . . JAMES M. DAVIS
Lead Carpenter . . . . MARK SPARKS
Labor Foreperson . . . . JOHN LEONE
Paint Supervisor . . . . THOMAS E. BROWN
Paint Forepersons . . . . ANDY SCUDIER
LAURENCE LAURENT
Production Painter . . . . DON ABBLETT
Greens Coordinator . . . . DAN GILLOOLY
Greens Foreperson . . . . KEITH P. BRAGG
First Company Rigging Grip . . . . . JEFF KLUTTZ
Second Company Rigging Grips . . OSCAR GOMEZ
MICHAEL L. GRADY
Chief Rigging Lighting Technicians . . . . . .
DENNIS "DJ" LOOTENS
SHAUN BREEDLOVE
Assistant Chief Rigging Lighting Technician . .
BRANCH M. BRUNSON
ELECTRICIANS
GORDY JORIAN   BLAKE HILL
GREG PATTERSON   BRIAN SKILTON
ROY GITTENS   KATIE NILSON
RAY GONZALEZ   RON NEWBURN
Boat Effects Designer . . . . PETER CHESNEY
Special Effects . . . . LARZ ANDERSON
Special Effects Crew (Florida) . . THOMAS KITTLE
DURK TYNDALL
MIKE ARBOGAST

Special Effects Crew (L.A.)   CHAD BAALBERGEN
JIM FREDBURG
ROLAND LOWE
TOM WARD
Image Engineering Coordinator . . . .
BLAINE CONVERSE
Marine Coordinator . . . . PHIL KINGRY
Transportation Coordinator . . . STEVE BRODSKY
Transportation Captains . . . . . . KEVIN C. SCOTT
RANDALL PETERSON
Additional Assistant Directors . . . . . . JILL MUSSER
SUSAN L. CARPENTER
Second Unit Assistant Director . . . .
ROBERT HUBERMAN
Special Atmospheric Effects   . . . . BOLAN JET AIR
Location Casting . . . . ELLEN JACOBY, C.S.A
Video Producer . . . . RICK WHITFIELD
Video Camera Operators . . . . JAY NEFCY
THOMAS L. ROWE
Video Technicians . . . . ROY BEAN
TOM SCHURKE
RICK TALMADGE
Computer Displays . . . . NEIL CLARK
Video Editor . . . . JIM SEVIN
Telecine . . . . PHIL VOSS
Video Assist Operators . . WILLIAM S. BYERS, JR.
VAN SCARBORO
Video Projection . . . .
AMERICAN HIGH DEFINITION
Post Production Supervisor ROSEMARY DORITY
Additional Film Editing . . . . KEVIN D. ROSS
Lightworks Assistants . . . . JOHN LEE
PADRAIC McKINLEY
Assistant Film Editors   MARIE-PIERRE RENAUD
PAULA LOURIE
BASIA OZERSKI
NOELLEEN WESTCOMBE
Apprentice Editors . . . . TODD FULKERSON
LIAM ANDERSON
Music Editor . . . . BUNNY ANDREWS
Sound Designer . . . . LEE SMITH
Supervising ADR Editor KARIN WHITTINGTON
Effects Editors . . . . RICK LISLE
PETER TOWNEND
Dialogue Editors . . . . TIM JORDAN
ANDREW PLAIN
Assistant Sound Editors . . . NICHOLAS BRESLIN
MAUREEN RODBARD-BEAN
Sound Apprentice . . . . RODNEY BERLING
Foley Walker . . . . JOHN SIMPSON
Foley Recordist . . . . JULIE PEARCE
ADR Mixer . . . . BOB BARON

Voice Casting . . . . BARBARA HARRIS
Re-Recording Mixers . . . . PHIL HEYWOOD
MARTIN OSWIN
Post-Production Facilities . . . .
SPECTRUM FILMS, SYDNEY
Sound Mixing Facilities . . SOUNDFIRM, SYDNEY
Production Coordinator . . . . JUDY PRITCHARD
Assistant Production Coordinators . . . .
J.M. BASCOM (L.A.)
RICHARD CHAPLA (Florida)
Travel Coordinator . . . . . . ADRIENNE VERGOS
Philip Glass Original Music Produced by . . .
KURT MUNKACSI
Unit Publicists . . . . DEBORAH SIMMRIN
SANDY OíNEILL
Extras Casting (L.A.) . . . . BILL DANCE CASTING
SANDY ALESSI
Casting Associates . . MEREDITH TUCKER (L.A.)
DANA McFADDEN (Florida)
Production Auditor . . . . CRYSTAL A. HAWKINS
Assistant Production Auditor . . . .
ANAMARIE C. GONZAGA
Auditing Assistants . . . . . NOLAN B. MEDRANO
HELENA M. RUIZ
JOAN ZULFER
Payroll . . . . ANTONIA PROSCIA
Construction Auditor . . PATRICK R. SIEMBIEDA
Assistant Production Auditors . . . .
MICHAEL J. MOSLEY
WANDA JOYCE STEPHENS
Seaside Liaison . . . . BETH FOLTA
Catering . . MICHELSON FOOD SERVICE, INC.
Craft Service . . . . CRAIG GLASSER
JOHN JAMES GEARY
Animals provided by . . . .
BIRDS AND ANIMALS, UNLIMITED
Animal Trainers . . . . CHERYL HARRIS
TAMMY BLACKBURN
Wescam provided by . . . . WESCAM USA
PRODUCTION ASSISTANTS
MARY BRUNNER   GENE GILLESPIE
ALOURA CHARLES   JEFF GROSS
JENNIFER COOK   JOSHUA MILNE
AMY DEAN   JACKSON PEEL
TIM DUTROW   MIKE TRIPLETT
MARK WALBAUM
Color Timer . . . . MIKE MILLIKEN
Negative Cutter . . . .
THERESA REPOLA MOHAMMED
Dolby Stereo Consultant . . . . . . STEVE MURPHY
Opticals by . . . . PACIFIC TITLE
Titles by . . CINEMA RESEARCH CORPORATION

Visual Effects Producer ...... JULIETTE YAGER
SPECIAL VISUAL EFFECTS by ..... CINESITE
Digital Visual Effects Supervisor .. BRAD KUEHN
Digital Visual Effects Producer ....
         ARIANA LINGENFELSER
Digital Effects Supervisor KEVIN LINGENFELSER
3D Supervisor .... JOE PASQUALE
Digital Compositor .... DAVID LINGENFELSER
Digital Artists .... TED ANDRE
         LAURA HANIGAN
CGI Animators .... MIEKO YOSHIDA
         GOKHAN KISACIKOGLU
         JASON WARDLE
         EDUARDO SILVA
         RICHARD KLEIN
         ERIC PENDER
Concept Matte Artist ...... ROGER KUPELIAN
Digital Effects Associate Producer ....
         RICHARD A. BENOIT
Rotoscope Supervisor .... KAREN KLEIN
Rotoscope Artist .... MARK LEWIS
Digital Technician Supervisor . TONY SGUEGLIA
Digital Imaging Technician ..... CHRIS REGAN
Digital Imaging Scheduler .... BRUCE BULLOCK
Digital Compositing by ....
     THE COMPUTER FILM COMPANY
   JANEK SIRRS   STELLA BOGH
   JANET YALE   DAVID FUHRER
  TRAVIS BAUMANN ERIC WEINSCHENK
         DYLAN CARTER
3D Matte Paintings by ... MATTE WORLD DIGITAL,
         Marin County, California
Visual Effects Supervisor ...... CRAIG BARRON
Executive in Charge of Production ....
         KRYSTYNA DEMKOWICZ
Visual Effects Producer .. MARTIN MATZINGER
Chief Digital Matte Artist .... CHRIS EVANS
Digital Matte Artists .... BRETT NORTHCUTT
         CAROLEEN GREEN
Digital Composite Supervisor .... PAUL RIVERA
Digital Compositor .... TODD R. SMITH
3D Modeler .... MORGAN TROTTER
3D Models & Textures .... TODD SIECHEN
Motion Control Photography ..... PATRICK LIN
First Company Grip .... PAUL SIEGEL
Effects Editorial .... KEN ROGERSON
Production Assistants .... BRIAN RINGSEIS
         ANDREW PICCONE
Tru-Talk Title Sequence Designed by .....
         IMAGINARY FORCES
Additional Visual Effects by .. AVAILABLE LIGHT EDS
         STIRBER VISUAL NETWORK

"PIANO SONATA NO. 11 IN A MAJOR (K331) (300)"
Third Movement: "Alla Turca"
by Wolfgang Amadeus Mozart
Performed by Wilhelm Kempff, Piano
Courtesy of Deutsche Grammophon Gesellschaft
mbH., Hamburg
by arrangement with PolyGram Film & TV Music

"THE BEGINNING"
"LIVING WATERS"
"ANTHEM—PART 1"
"ANTHEM—PART 2"
"OPENING"
Written & Performed by Philip Glass
Courtesy of Nonesuch Records
by arrangement with Warner Special Products

"TWENTIETH CENTURY BOY"
by Marc Bolan
Performed by The Big Six
Courtesy of Vinyl Japan UK Limited

"PIANO CONCERTO NO. 1 IN E MINOR, OPUS 11"
Second Movement: "Romance—Larghetto"
by Frederic Chopin
Performed by Artur Rubinstein
Stanislaw Skrowaczewski, Conductor
Courtesy of BMG Classics/RCA Victor

"SCALES TO AMERICA"
by David Hirschfelder
Performed by David Hirschfelder & Orchestra
Mary Doumany, Harp
Conducted by Ricky Edwards
Courtesy of Philips Classics
by arrangement with PolyGram Film & TV Music

"HORN CONCERTO NO. 1 IN D MAJOR (K412)"
First Movement: Allegro
by Wolfgang Amadeus Mozart
Performed by Philharmonia Baroque Orchestra
Nicholas McGegan, Conductor
Lowell Greer, Soloist
Courtesy of Harmonia Mundi France
by arrangement with Source/Q

"LOVE IS JUST AROUND THE CORNER"
by Leo Robin & Lewis Gensler
Performed by Jackie Davis
Courtesy of Capitol Records
under license from EMI-Capitol Music Special
Markets

"Wiegenlied (Lullaby)"
by Johannes Brahms

"Underground"
Written & Performed by Burkhard Dallwitz
Courtesy of Media World Pty. Ltd

"Father Kolbe's Preaching"
by Wojciech Kilar
Performed by Orchestre Philharmonique
National de Pologne
Kazimierz Kord, Conductor
Courtesy of Editions Jade

Filmed on location at
Seaside, Florida
The Producers wish to express their appreciation for
the generous cooperation of :
Robert and Daryl Davis and the community of
Seaside

The Sandestin Beach Hilton Resort
Okaloosa/Ft. Walton Community College
Walton, Bay, and Okaloosa Counties, Florida
Carillon Beach, Florida—a village by the sea

Printed on Eastman Kodak Film
Color by Deluxe
Filmed with Panavision Cameras and Lenses
Digital Dolby Stereo In Selected Theatres
DTS Digital Sound In Selected Theatres

No. 34959 (MPAA Globe)
IATSE "Bug"
Motion Picture Association of America

ABOUT THE AUTHORS

ANDREW NICCOL, a New Zealander, wrote *The Truman Show* before turning his hand to directing. *Gattaca,* also an original screenplay by Niccol, was his feature film directing debut—a science fiction drama about genetic discrimination.

Academy Award® nominee **PETER WEIR** previously directed *Witness, Dead Poet's Society, Picnic at Hanging Rock, Gallipoli, The Year of Living Dangerously, The Mosquito Coast,* and *Fearless.* He lives in Australia.